To H.

ACKNOWLEDGEMENTS

Xiangdong Primary School was the scene of my first successes. The staff and teachers gave me the grounding and confidence to excel.

Beijing Middle School Attached to Railway Institute had a team of teachers and an environment that allowed me to develop my interests and to grow.

Beijing University of Aeronautics and Astronautics had professors that took an interest in my potential and had the kind of English language and literature program that introduced me to the best of the written culture.

Beijing Today was my training ground for the rigors of journalism. I learned at the side of experts, both supervisors and colleagues, who took the time and patience to teach me to navigate the shoals of real-life investigative reporting and features writing.

The University of Sheffield Department of Journalism Studies provided a testing ground for my understanding of English society, and the professors and fellow students were dedicated guides along that roadway.

McGill University Department of Graduate Studies was rich in courses and mentors that both informed me and led me to challenges for my further development.

The Sauvé Scholars Foundation was my generous sponsor and home for almost a year, and aside from the richness of its program, provided me with caring advisors and peers who will remain friends for life.

The Montreal Chinese community welcomed me and integrated me into their cultural and social life, and made me feel at home so far away from home.

The good citizens of Sheffield, Barnsley, Leeds, and Doncaster in the English Midlands were overwhelming with their hospitality to this stranger in their midst. From home cooking to guided walking tours to generous counseling, their collective and individual warmth made a challenging stay more pleasant.

And special thanks to my parents, my aunts and their families, for the richness of experience that nourished me, encouraged an early self-reliance and provided the basis for many of my stories.

This book is particularly to thank my grandmother, Wu Fengying, who died when I was 13.

北京小孩

BEIJING KID
WEI SU

CONTENTS

1

北京小孩

1

TIGER

I had two dogs when I was at middle school. There were many times that I wanted to kick them severely just because I felt extremely angry and it was the time when they were coming just to be my companions. The good thing is that I never really kicked them as I knew that I would regret having done this to them.

Before I had the two dogs I had another dog. I do not know who left it in front of my house. My mother was opposed to the idea that I let it stay in our house. My father did not make any comment. I called him Tiger. I used to play with him every day. I only kept him for the spring and summer before my mother killed him in the autumn.

北京小孩

2

Because Tiger was big, as big as a donkey, I used to sit on his back. I was about nine years old. He liked grass very much. I used to pick a lot of grass for him. And I asked my grandmother to make a hat for him. He liked wearing the hat and sitting beside me. Sometimes I played tricks with him. I put the hat on his tail and asked him to get the hat. First he walked slowly and then more slowly, and suddenly he began to run to get hold of the hat. I used to sit near the door and watch him running to get the hat on his tail.

My father used to cut my hair as short as a boy's. Each time when Tiger saw my father with the shaver he always ran to my grandmother to get a piece of cloth which would be put around my neck. When my father was shaving my head, Tiger usually sat beside my feet looking at me. I used to tease him. I said to him, "I will shave your hair." I do not know if he could understand me. But I do remember he looked at me, and pretended to run and then used his tail to sweep my hair on the floor everywhere. After my father cut my hair, I always ran after Tiger with the cloth in my hands. And I always succeeded in putting the cloth around his neck. I liked seeing him running, jumping and waving his tail with the cloth. His hair was thick, soft and black. I liked to touch his neck, head and back.

I used to let him have whatever I had. I like watermelon and he shared the watermelon with me. I like peaches and he shared peaches with me. He was so clever that he could peel the peach and leave the core clean. I like fish and he shared fish with me. I like rice and he shared rice with me. Everyday when I had meals with my grandmother he always came to me and sat beside me, raising his head and looking at me. My grandmother said he was spoiled by me as I normally fed him from the table.

But he would never come to the table if my mother was there and my father was not. My mother once kicked him severely. It was a day with heavy rain. I did not know what happened to him. When I came home he was lying in his shelter and moaning. I went to him and asked him what was wrong. He just moaned and moaned. I saw tears in his eyes. I tried to touch his neck but he avoided me. He looked at his stomach and I found it was very very red, purple and blue. I put my hands on his stomach and he avoided my touch as if electricity suddenly passed through him. I then put my hand on his head and he used his tongue to lick my hand and my face. My mother suddenly appeared behind me and Tiger shook.

I asked my mother what had happened. She simply said Tiger stole food from the kitchen. I did not believe what she said. I asked my grandmother. She told me later that Tiger was in the kitchen when my mother came back from school. She asked Tiger to come to her and then kicked him. My grandmother said she heard Tiger cry and when she rushed to the yard she saw Tiger

3

was like a bowl thrown to the wall. She said she asked my mother what happened and my mother said Tiger stole food from the kitchen.

Tiger died before he really recovered. It was the time that the Beijing government decided to have all the unregistered dogs collected. I remember it was a very very hot day in the early days of September. My mother called me to help her. I saw that she had tied a rope on our big date tree in the garden. I asked her what she was going to do. She said we must kill Tiger. I asked her why. She said she did not want us to be fined and if Tiger was found by the government as not being registered they would kill him too. And she said we should not spend money to register him. My mother said it was better that Tiger was killed by us. I said to my mother that no one would know that we had a dog if Tiger did not bark. I said Tiger was very very quiet so no one would find him. I also said I could keep him in my room and I promised that I would not let him bark and would not let others find him. My mother did not agree. She said she had talked to my father and they both thought killing Tiger would be the best solution.

Tiger seemed to know what was going to happen. He was very very calm. My mother put the rope around his neck as he looked at me, trying to give his tongue to me. My mother asked me to stand beside her in case Tiger might jump. She got a barrel of water and used a big spoon to get the water into Tiger's mouth. At the same time she tied the rope around Tiger. Tiger raised his head, cried and looked at me. I did not dare to walk to him. His eyes were full of despair. He closed his eyes

北京小孩

4

slowly and slowly. Tears came down from his eyes. He kept his head pointed towards me. But I never moved to him. He cried. A few minutes later he stopped crying.

Then my mother loosened the rope. She tied up Tiger to the date tree and skinned Tiger. We had Tiger for our next day's dinner.

I thought I would cry. But I did not. I ate Tiger and from then on I began to eat dog's meat. Now I love dog's meat. It is the most delicious meat that I have ever had.

5

北京小孩

2

JUNE 4, 1989

I was eleven in the year of 1989 on June 4. For me, that year, that month and that incident is a puzzle. I do not think I will be able to find the truth. But it is the year that I started to feel that the world is not as simple as I thought.

In my memory the whole incident started with the death of Hu Yaobang, a former Party General Secretary. I remember that the schools in Beijing gave the day off for Hu's death ceremony. So did my school, Xiangdong

Primary School. And my teacher asked us to write something about the ceremony. Everything seemed normal until one day the news said some university students let themselves go on hunger strike at Tian'anmen Square. First it was just occasionally reported in the news, later it was reported everyday and it took over the newscast at every news break, and eventually all the programming itself.

Later some of the students refused to take any water and the International Red Cross became involved. Everyday the news said more university students fainted and were sent to hospital. Everyday I could hear the ambulance sirens screaming on the streets and I could see the ambulances running through the city. And everyday more press conferences were held and shown on TV. And everyday I saw the students with intravenous needles lying in the mobile beds talking to the government officials at the press conference and everyday I saw some of the students at the press conference just faint and lose consciousness. And I remember my mother said, "Poor child, poor child," while she was watching the press conference. And everyday there was more news saying that the local Beijingers donated money to get medicine for the university students, and for delivering food to Tian'anmen Square.

I remember one afternoon my mother came home much earlier. She said to my father that her students went to Tian'anmen Square to support the university students. She was a teacher at Beijing No. 105 Middle School at that time. And her students were aged fourteen.

I remember my mother said she went to Tian'anmen Square too because she wanted to get her students back to her classroom. Her school did not allow students to go to Tian'anmen Square. She said when she met her students they told her that they cried when they saw the university students. And she said she felt her heart went out to the university students and she said she did not understand why the government did not do anything to help the university students and let them go back to university. And I remember she said her students told her that when they were about to give some money for the university students and were about to join them, the university students said to them to go back to their classroom, and they said to her students to cherish the opportunity to learn as much as possible so in the future they could build a much stronger China. I remember my mother asked my father if he knew what was happening and my father said to my mother clearly, "Something is going to happen. Do not say anything. Just do the job that you are supposed to do."

At the end of May, the news said the workers in Beijing announced their support for the university students and then workers in Shanghai announced their support. I remember my mother was eager to go to Tian'anmen Square again but was stopped by my father. "Stay at home. Do the job that you are supposed to do. The situation is not clear," he said seriously. At that time my school let us go home at noon and asked us to bring a note from our parents to show the time we got home and what we did afterwards. I remember everyday the teachers at the primary school talked about the

北京小孩

9

university students going on hunger strike but they always kept silent when we were around.

One day when my mother turned on TV, Zhao Ziyang, the General Secretary for the Party at that time, appeared at Tian'anmen Square. And I remember he cried when he stood at Tian'anmen Square surrounded by the university students. I was surprised how such a big man could cry in public. And I remember the first sentence that I heard from him was, "My dear children, I am sorry. I am too late. I am too late. I should have come to see you earlier." And I remember all the people around him looked sad and the students cried.

When my father came back my mother told him, "Zhao Ziyang came out. Zhao Ziyang came out. He was at Tian'anmen Square." My father interrupted her. "Do not think it is a good sign. Something is going to happen soon. Stay at home. Do the job that you are supposed to do." My mother still wanted to say something, but my father turned away.

I remember just before June 1 my school took us to the Children's Activity Center near Xizhimen. It is on the way to Tian'anmen Square. I saw many people riding their bikes or taking trucks, holding flags. I remember when they saw us they clapped their hands and asked us, "Are you going to Tian'anmen Square? Let's go together!" And then they waved the flags. I remember they were the flags for the Party and the country. I remember my classmates and I, even my teachers were excited. We waved to these people.

On June 1 I heard my mother and our neighbors saying something about soldiers, guns, tanks and the

北京小孩

10

army. "They are in Deshengmen," one of my cousins said. Deshengmen, right on the second ring road, is the place where the ancient emperors welcomed his victorious armies from the wars. It is just outside Tian'anmen Square. "Really? What are they for?" my mother asked. "I do not know." "Do you want to go and have a look?" My cousin's mother was afraid and was about to stop her daughter and my mother. But my mother and my cousin still went and they took me along.

It was a sunny day. The sunshine was very strong. Right after turning on the road to the Arrow Tower of Deshengmen, I saw several lines of green trucks. Some of the trucks were covered with thick green cloth. I wondered what was inside. The local residents were standing close to the trucks where the soldiers were sitting inside. They all wore helmets and dark green uniforms with their hands holding machine guns and ammo belts and different sizes of shell boxes. No matter how hard the local residents tried to make these soldiers speak, the soldiers mostly kept silent. I remember a man beside me asking a solider, "When did you arrive?" "Last night." "Why did you come here?" The soldier did not answer. "Where did you come from?" The soldier had no expression on his face while holding his gun tightly. "Which army do you belong to?" The solider still did not answer. "He won't tell you. It is a secret." I heard someone say this.

I looked at these soldiers. They were very young, none older than any university student, I guessed. They were very very hot as they were sweating and their uniforms were wet. But they still sat straight. "Uncle, are you going to shoot the students?" I asked them. I did not know where I got the impression that they were going to shoot the students. I remember the soldier whom the man asked questions of looked at me and said, "I am not allowed to speak to anyone." "Little girl, we know the students are good and mean good. We won't shoot them. But we are soldiers and we need to do whatever we are asked to do," someone said to me. I looked in that direction. It was an officer, thin and dark colored. He bent down, put his hand on my shoulder and looked at me, "Whom do you come with?" "My mother." "Tell your mother to bring you home. Be good." He then stood up and left.

On the night of June 4 my parents and I were watching TV. It was a detective series and normally it only had one act per day. But it was the first time that four acts were shown. I was so happy that I could see the ending of the detective story. I remember I said to my father, "I wished it could happen every day. It is really good. But why was it not shown before? Why?" My father looked irritated and he did not answer me. Then there was a line on the bottom of the screen, "All the residents should not go out tonight. You must stay at home." I asked my father what it meant. He did not say anything but his eyebrows twisted. "Something is going to happen. Something is going to happen," he said. I did not really understand. I thought no one would go out and miss the opportunity to watch the four acts and to miss the ending. And suddenly the screen went blank. Several big characters came on the screen, "All the

北京小孩
12

residents must stay at home. All the residents must stay at home." And the lights at home went off. I felt something had happened.

The following morning was very very quiet.

And it was also quiet for the following days. I did not go to school at all. I was told by my parents that I should not go to school. And they did not go to work. I was puzzled. But I was happy that I had a few days off. I had expected that there would be more TV series showing four acts again. But it never happened.

北京小孩

13

One day I heard our neighbors talk about killing. "There were holes on the walls and the windows were hit. I cannot believe this," said one of our neighbors who had relatives living near Tian'anmen Square. "Do not say it any more. Do not say it any more," said her husband. I felt it was strange. I asked my mother. She asked me to ask my father. I asked my father. He did not answer me but left the TV on all day. I first heard the term "anti-revolutionary riot" but I had no idea what it really meant. In my memory anything anti-revolutionary happened before the liberation of China and right after the liberation. And I was surprised to hear the news say that the university students were used to attack and throw down the Communist rule. I was surprised that there were so many people, including professors and students, who were wanted and arrested by the Communist Party as the ones who conspired or assisted to throw down the Communist Party rule. And some of them were the ones that I saw having intravenous needles at the press conference.

北京小孩

One morning my cousin said to my mother that the army was stationed at Beijing Exhibition Museum and Beijing Capital Stadium on the other side of the Gaoliang River where we lived. My mother went to the river bank and I went to the river bank. There were crowds from all the households in my area, Toudui Village, on the river bank. "Look at the tanks." "See the guns." People stood on their toes and stretched their necks, pointing to each other. I saw a wave of dark green cross the river. From then on, every morning and evening I could hear the soldiers shouting loudly during their training, I could hear them stomping on the ground, and I could see them running in rows, and I could see them practicing with their shining guns. I was curious but was also scared.

I remember the first time when I went back to school my classmates were talking about guns shooting and tanks running through the city. And so were the teachers. But on the second day each of us was asked to buy a brochure about the soldiers being killed by the anti-revolutionary people. And it talked about how these soldiers were killed, with their stomachs being opened and everything inside taken out and twisted into a knot, hanging on an overpass, or a group of soldiers being beaten with heavy injuries and then burnt to death. For me, these were all stories and I needed these stories as I, a Young Pioneer, like any other Young Pioneer, needed to do some writing about the braveness of these soldiers.

In the following days the news was mainly about soldiers being killed without shooting at the people, followed by the announcement that the soldiers needed food, and then the announcement of the Party members making political mistakes, including Zhao. And at that time there were a few of the same officials on TV and I remember I did not like them at all. They did not look like good people and my mother scolded me because I told her this.

My mother was criticized by her school for not stopping her students from going to Tian'anmen Square. I remember my father said to her, "Now you know that I was right to tell you not to do anything. How can you still be a Party member without knowing the Party's intention?"

Around the middle of June the primary school organized us to bring rice, watermelons, and peaches to the army stationed at Beijing Capital Stadium. And I remember, as the head for all the Young Pioneers at the primary school, I was asked to write a letter to the soldiers to thank them for protecting the country, the people and their property.

And I put a bright red scarf on a senior officer to show the love and respect to him and all the soldiers.

北京小孩

15

3

MILK

I do not remember when I started drinking milk for my breakfast.

I remember when I was at primary school I had milk with one egg in it for my breakfast. It is my grandmother's favorite. After she came back from her morning walk along the Gaoliang River in front of my house and from getting grass from the wild land near Beijing Zoo for the chicken that we kept, and if I was still at home, she would make breakfast for me. She poured the milk into a pot, rinsed the bottle with water and poured the water into the milk, turned on the cooker, and when the milk started to boil, she broke an egg and put the egg in. Then she turned down the cooker and waited for a few minutes. Then she got a small bowl, put some sugar in the bowl, poured in the milk, and then used a spoon to pick up the egg and put it into the bowl.

There was always a little bit of milk left in the pot. She always asked me to have the left milk in the pot first. She used to tell me that the skin of milk in the pot was the most nutritious. I listened to her and used my index finger to clean out the pot, and put it into my grandmother's mouth. She tried to avoid it but never succeeded. I then used my index finger to clean out the pot again and again until it became shiny and I put my finger with whatever I had gotten out into my mouth. The taste was really nice. And it is a habit I have kept till now. I remember I always said to my grandmother that we did not need to wash the pot as it was clean enough. She always laughed, nodded and turned on the tap to wash the pot.

Normally I did not have time to have the milk with egg as my mother always said to me that I should leave for school as early as possible. So I could only have a sip of the milk but had to run as my mother said I was already late. My grandmother always asked me to eat the egg but I did not have the time.

Later my grandmother started to put the bowl of milk with the egg into a big pot with cold water. She said the milk would become cool soon and it would give me the time to drink the milk and leave for school earlier. But I remember that most times either I had to leave for school before my grandmother came back or I just did not have the time for the milk to be boiled.

I remember we had a pre-paid card to collect the milk. Every afternoon I took the card with me and went to a grocery store to get a bottle of milk after giving them the empty bottle. Most times I went there with my grandmother. And we stood in a line waiting for the milkman to deliver the milk to the store. At that time it was the only grocery store for the 300 households from my area, Toudui Village.

My grandmother stood behind me firmly in the line and did not say anything. The empty bottle was as clean as a new one, no stains but clear. Years later when I did my chemistry experiments in a lab I knew that the cleanest tubes should be the ones that are clear, without any water. And I always remember the empty bottle.

When we were standing in the line I always played with the bottle. It was like a vase though it was not big enough to put in more than three flowers. It was thick but I could see my grandmother's face through the bottle. The color of the bottle was light green. It was green but it was like the green of the clearest creek. And the bottom was extremely thick and it seemed there were several layers of glass. I asked my grandmother why the bottle was so thick and she said because I might break it. I laughed and she laughed. I put the bottle in front of my eyes and I saw her laughter lasting for a long time.

People who went to the grocery store all had small bags made from hard plastic in which to put their

北京小孩

bottles of milk. But we did not have one. We either put the milk in a plastic bag or just held it with our hands. And for those who had the hard plastic bags they put the card in their bag, but for us we always held it in our hands.

北京小孩

I remember one day I went to the grocery store to get the milk. My grandmother was not at home. My aunt, my father's elder sister, had taken my grandmother to her place. When I was at the grocery store I could not find the card. I told the milkman that I might have lost it. He told me to try to remember where I had been. I walked all the way back to my home and all the way back to the grocery store. But I could not find it. I was scared as I knew it was the beginning of the month and we needed the card to get the milk. I cried when I was back at the grocery store. I told the milkman that I could not find it. He said to me it was alright. He said he could still give me a bottle of milk. He knew that I was the girl that always came to get milk with an old woman, and always played with the cleanest bottle. He asked me to give him the bottle. I suddenly realized it was not in my hands. I remembered that I put the bottle and the card in a plastic bag. But where were they? I said to him I could not remember where I put the bottle as well and I said I could not remember what had happened and how such things could happen. He said he still had a bottle of milk for me. He said he knew me. He said next day I just needed to bring the bottle back.

I began to smile. And as I was leaving I saw him getting ten cents from his own pocket and put it into the boxes where the empty bottles were standing. I turned to him and said to him that I would get the money and I did not need the milk for today. He laughed and said, "Do not worry. Go home now. Your grandmother must be worried about you."

I put the bottle of milk in the plastic bag. It was getting dark. I started to run. At the last corner close to my home I fell over. I saw the bottle flying out of the bag and the snowy white milk spreading everywhere. The sound when the bottle hit the ground was rifle-sharp. The milk spilled out in violent waves. I did not get up but kept staring at the milk coming out from the bottle and the bag. I saw the bottle was lying with the lid still on it. I knew that the bottle was broken.

When I was back I had nothing in my hands. I told my mother what had happened. And I showed her the bottle, actually two parts of the bottle. She said how dare could I be so careless. She said I was useless. She asked me to throw out the broken bottle. But I did not. I washed the pieces because I wanted them to be clean and I knew and believed that someone could fix it. My mother did not allow me to do this. She said clearly that I must throw the bottle-pieces away. And this time I listened to her. I threw the bottle into the garbage. And I remember it was there for several days.

On the following morning my grandmother came back. She had a hard plastic bag in her hand. She said we could go to get the milk with the bag. And I cried. I told her what had happened. She said to me, "Do not cry. It is just a bottle of milk. Did you hurt yourself? Let me see if you have hurt yourself." It was the first time that I remembered to check myself. Yes I had bruises on

北京小孩

21

my knees. And I started to feel the hurt. My grandmother said I should clean the wounds as soon as possible otherwise they would be infected.

We did not go to collect the milk any more as my mother said to me that she cancelled the milk and got the rest of the money back. My mother said that no one in the family could drink milk and it would be better if we used the milk money on something else. Then we did not have any milk until I was at university. Then I could get some milk with the pocket money that my father gave to me. And I started to have milk again every morning. I always heat the milk on a cooker. I always make one liter or half liter of milk in a pot. I always clean the pot with my index finger and put it into my mouth. And I always wait until the milk cools and drink it up. My mother says I should not have that much milk every day. She says it is not good for me. She laughs at me when she sees that I suck my finger with milk on it. She does not understand why I do it and she asks me why. She says I am like an uneducated person. I do not know the reason but I know that I want to have the milk every day and I want to have the skin of the milk with my index finger.

We never had the chance to use the hard plastic bag to collect milk. It was a hand-made one with blue and white stripes. I never asked my grandmother where she got it. And I kept it in my room for a pencil bag.

And it took a whole month to recover from the bruises because of the infection. I still have the marks on my knees.

4

KATYDIDS

I t is the season that vendors ride bikes, passing on many roads and alleys in Beijing, to sell the katydids. I am tempted to get the katydids in small bamboo cases, but I decided not to.

The first time that I kept katydids was when I spent a summer vacation with my aunt in the rural area of Beijing. She is my mother's elder sister. Before I started to travel alone as a middle school student I always spent my summers with the families of my mother's two elder sisters. Both of them are peasants, living in Changping District, north of Beijing. And each of them had a huge field to grow corn or wheat.

I remember on one afternoon my cousin took me to the field as she needed to get rid of the weeds and collect the corn. On the way to the field we passed a watermelon patch and I heard some strange clear and loud sounds. I asked my cousin what they were. She told me they were the sound of katydids. She said to me if I was careful I could catch some katydids. She told me they were green with big bellies. I was so curious that I said to her that I wanted to get some. She told me the best time was noon when it was very hot.

So on the following day at noon my cousin took me back to the watermelon patch. She got two straw hats, one for me and the other for her. I asked her why I should wear a hat. She said because I was a city girl and my skin was very delicate. I remember her skin was very dark and it was exactly the same as the tanned skin these days. Her hair was brown but long. She made a knot of her hair and put it into her hat.

She hushed me to be quiet. I followed her. She bent over, listened attentively, and then walked quietly but fast to one side of the patch. I could hear the sounds made by the katydid were getting louder and louder. I felt they were right under my feet. I shouted to her, "Did you see them? Let me catch them!" She stood back up and looked at me disappointedly with her arms stretched in front of her legs and hands facing upward. Suddenly there was completely quiet. I knew that I should not shout.

My cousin and I stood for a few minutes in the sun. I asked her if we could still get some katydids. She hushed me. Then the clear and sharp sound came. First there was only one, and it was broken. Then there was another one and it was becoming continuous. I looked at my cousin, wondering if we should start now. She did not look at me at all. I then decided to be quiet. We still waited, standing in the sun. I was sweating. The sweat came from my hat, flowing through my forehead, my eyebrows into my eyes and then down to my chin. I looked at my cousin again. She still stood without any movement. Sweat came out of her hat. It was like the crystals on her dark skin. I wondered if I had the same sweat.

北京小孩

25

I lost patience. I was ready to move as I heard the sounds were everywhere in the patch. And I was sure there must be one katydid near where I was standing. I lifted my right foot and was about to move. My cousin pulled me back and I could not keep my balance. I was pulled back to her body and she lost her balance and fell on a watermelon with the clear sound of the watermelon being cracked. And I was falling onto her body. The red juice and fruit meat of the watermelon spread everywhere, her blouse, her hat and my skirt and my hat. The black shining seeds jumped into my hands, her hands, my face and her face. The red juice was flowing to another watermelon and I cracked another watermelon when I tried to support myself against the fall. I had all of my left hand into the watermelon. I looked at my cousin and she looked at me. We burst into laughter.

An old topless man, wearing the same kind of hat that my cousin and I wore, waving a bamboo leaf fan, looked at us from a hut on the other side of the watermelon patch. "What are you doing there?" he shouted, putting the fan over his head. "Let's run," I said to my cousin. "No," said my cousin. "Elder uncle, it is me. This is my cousin from Beijing. She has never seen a katydid and I wanted to get one for her. But we damaged your watermelons. I am sorry about this," my cousin said while getting up. I saw watermelon pieces were all over her trousers. "I see. Why didn't you say this earlier? It is easy. Let me get it for you. Do not stand in the sun. You girls have delicate skin." he said. My cousin took us to his hut.

I saw there were many bamboo cases and in each case there was one big insect with a big belly. "Have the watermelon, have the watermelon," said the old man. He picked up one watermelon under his feet, with a big long sharp and shining knife in his hand. With the tip of the knife touching the skin of the watermelon, the watermelon split into two halves by itself. Inside was the fresh red watermelon meat decorated with the round tiny black seeds. He then cut each half of the watermelon into another four pieces, picked one and gave it to me. "Eat." "No. Thanks." "Eat. Do not be shy. I do not have anything to entertain you. You are a city girl and you must have had a lot of food that I have never heard of but my watermelon is much better that the ones that you have had. Eat it." He pushed the watermelon right into my mouth. I took it and had a big bite. It was so juicy and so fresh. Within several seconds I finished this piece. '"Is it good?" he asked me. I nodded as I had all the watermelon in my mouth. My cousin laughed. "You did not spit out the seeds?" she said and laughed. "Really? I did not notice," I said. "One more?" asked the old man. "No. Thanks." "Do not be shy." He then pushed another piece into my mouth.

While I was having the watermelon, he got a dozen bamboo cases with katydids, tied them with a straw, and put them into my cousin's hands. "Take them with you. I have nothing to give to our guest except these." "No. It is too much. One is enough," said my cousin. "No. The more you have the more pleasant the sound you have. Take them." He then put another two watermelons in a big bamboo basket. "Take them as well," he said. "No. It is too much," said my cousin and I "Do not say that. Do you want me to bring them to your home?" said the old man. "Go, go." He pushed us out of his hut when my cousin and I tried to leave the watermelons. "Do not forget to give a small piece of the watermelon skin to the katydids," he shouted when we were walking away from his field. I looked back. He was waving his hat at me, with a grin on his face. And his skin was even darker than my cousin's.

In the evening my aunt cut up one of the watermelons for us and it was even sweeter than the one that I had in the hut. I asked my aunt about the old man. She said his wife died in the early 1970s during the Cultural Revolution and left a son at the age of four for him. He did not get remarried as he was worried that his second wife might not treat his son well. He supported his son to go to school by growing watermelons and

北京小孩

selling katydids. And now his son got married and moved into town and seldom went to see him. My aunt said his son said it was a shame that his father was a watermelon grower and katydid vendor. She said his son tried to stop him from doing this by threatening to cut him off. And he cried and begged his son that he could not leave the watermelons and katydids. My aunt said his son liked keeping katydids when he was a child, but not now. She then let out a big sigh.

That night I woke up several times looking at the katydids. And on the following morning I went to the watermelon patch again. But the old man was not there. I waited till noon but he was still not there. When I went back my aunt told me that he had a stroke last night. And this morning when people found him he was in the watermelon patch with the cases of katydids in his hands. He had lost consciousness.

For the rest of the days that I stayed with my aunt I asked her several times about him. And my aunt said he was in hospital. I said it was good that nothing serious really happened. "It is good but it would be better if he had died," said my aunt. "He can't speak and can't move. He has lost the ability to look after himself." I did not ask if his son would look after him or not and I did not want to ask.

The day before I went back to my own home I brought all the katydids to the watermelon patch. Weeds there were very high. And there were not many watermelons left. The hut was full of dust and almost all the cases of katydids were gone. I opened the cases that he gave to me and left.

北京小孩

5

MOTHER AND I

My mother seldom went out with me. I only remember that she used to take me for trips during the summer vacations when I was at primary school. These trips were organized by her school. My father paid for all the trips for me.

When I was in middle school my mother said to me she would not go on any trips with me. She said she was too old and there was nothing that we could share. So I started to travel alone and she started taking the trips organized by her school alone. I remember there were several times that my father tried to stop my mother from going on trips alone. He used to ask her either to bring me with her or to stay at home. And each time it ended up with my mother crying. And I was always the one that told my father that he should let my mother go. And I was always the one that was complained about by my mother. She used to say it was because of me that she could not do a lot of things.

She used to say that it was because of me that she put on weight, from 55 to 90 kilos, although she lost 20 kilos since I was born. She used to say that it was because of me that she had an abortion some time after I was born. The year I was born was the year that the Chinese government made a decision to have a one-child policy. It was a boy. My mother told me she also had miscarriages three times before I was born. They were all boys. And she used to say because of me she had a terrible side-effect from my birth. She said to me the doctors at Haidian Hospital where she had the operation had to put tubes into her stomach through her nose to pump the air out. She used to say because of me my father and my grandfather asked her to eat a lot of unsalted ribs and chicken because they wanted her to breastfeed me. I remember my grandmother told me that I was raised on rice soup.

I know there were a lot of things that I could not do that would have made my mother proud of me. She used to tell me one girl from my primary school could read several thousand Chinese characters and write poems before she went to school. And my mother said I did not like to study at all. She said when I was a toddler I showed no interest in books at all. She said I always scratched on or tore off pages from her books.

I know that my mother used to ask me to write diaries everyday but I could not as I had no interest. She used to ask me to practice handwriting. I did try but could not keep on doing it. She said that my handwriting was like the mess made by a dog. She said I had no persistence.

北京小孩

She wanted me to learn to dance but found out that I had no sense of rhythm. She wanted me to learn piano but decided that my fingers were too short. She wanted me to learn violin but decided that I made sounds like a chicken whose neck was being squeezed. She then sent me to learn piano accordion at The People's Liberation Army Art School which I kept going to for six years but never touched afterwards. My mother could not understand why I was so clumsy in music - she is good at dancing and singing but I am not. She said when I sang the wolf would come. She could not understand why I could not enjoy learning a musical instrument when I had the chance. She said to me if she were me she would probably learn all the music instruments.

She wanted me to be a good basketball player, volleyball player and a good runner. But I couldn't. I could not hit the basket and I could not jump high enough to stop others. She said to me she was the center and also the forward in her school's basketball and volleyball teams in Changping District, north of Beijing. I can run fast but I could not do long distance running. She said to me she did well in the 100m, 200m, 400m

北京小孩

and long distance running. I felt there were a lot of things in which I could not compare well with her.

She used to say that I was very unsociable. She said I did not know how to meet people and how to talk to people. I do not know if she is right or not. I know that I am not a party person and I do not like to socialize with people. However sometimes I can easily interact with people whether they are the higher-up ones or the low class ones such as the dustmen and the doormen.

I remember that my mother was always the center of attention of any party or gatherings. She was very confident even when people made fun of her. But I could never be. I cannot tell if people tend to hurt me by the jokes that they tell.

I remember that I once asked my mother why she never held my hand, hugged me and kissed me which I saw that a mother did to her daughter when I was sixteen. I remember my mother said to me she did not think it was necessary.

I remember when I was a child there were times when I fell over and I cried. My mother never came to me. I did not expect her to help me stand up but I wish she could have just smiled at me. I am sure that just one smile would have been enough to cheer me up.

I remember one day I got two ice popsicles, one for me and the other for my mother. And I fell over when I was crossing the road. I held up the ice popsicles as I did not want to lose them or let them get dirty. I got dust on my skirt. When I gave one of the ice popsicles to my mother she simply asked me what happened. After I explained it to her, she said she could not understand why I was always so clumsy. I was around five years old.

I remember that my mother seldom brought me or picked me up from school when I was at primary school. She was against the idea. I did not feel anything strange though I really wanted her to be at the gate so I could run to her, like all the other children. But I knew that I should not expect it.

My mother is too keen on me being independent. A few days before I went to the University of Sheffield, England, to do my master's degree, I asked her and my father if they were going to see me off at the airport. She said I could take an airport shuttle. My father said it would be very difficult for me and he said maybe my cousin could take me to the airport. My mother said she could not go with me as she was teaching. I was disappointed. I told my father I really wanted to see them. I did not know what happened between my parents. One day before I left my father told me that both of them would go to the airport but they had to leave immediately once we got there.

Last year around Christmas, I sent an email to my parents telling them that I wanted to go home for my break. My mother said to me, "Do not come back. It costs money. We do not have the money for you. We have already spent too much money on you." I felt I was being thrown out. And I cried.

This year when I knew the date when I would be back to Beijing from Montreal I sent my parents an email, asking them if they could meet me at the airport. Their first email response was, "Your father and I do not have time. You can take the airport shuttle or you can take a taxi if you want." I replied by saying that I did not have Chinese money. A few days later they replied to me by saying," We will meet you at the airport but I have classes in the afternoon." Anyway it is always good to see my parents. And when I arrived at Beijing Capital International Airport the first person that I saw was my father. Actually he called out to me first. And I saw his eyes getting red. My mother did not turn up until a few minutes later.

北京小孩

34

Since I have been in Shanghai, I have phoned my parents several times. Most times my father answered. One was picked up by my mother. She did not talk to me. Instead she passed it to my father. I heard her say, "It is your daughter."

Now I rent an apartment near Taikang Road, the artistic street. And I am completely independent. I am nobody's daughter at all.

6

GRANDMOTHER

My grandmother and I were very close to each other. But my grandmother is the only one I really hurt. And I knew what I said and what I did would hurt her but I still did it and did it purposely.

I do not remember when I first lost my temper with her and why I acted terribly to her. I only remember I said to her, "This is not your home. You belong to your own family, the Wu family. This is the Su family. You are not my father's real mother. You are my father's stepmother. Go back to your own home." And each time my grandmother walked leaning against the wall with her bound feet, her head lowered, and she pushed her hand against wall. I know that I felt she was crying though she always cried quietly. People say when I cry I am like my grandmother, crying quietly and with tears coming out in big drops and then in streams.

北京小孩

I remember there were a couple of times my grandmother asked me where she could go. "I had nowhere to go. This is my home. I will never leave my home," she said firmly. I sneered, "Get your bedding and clothes. Leave my house. It is not my business where you go. You go. You must go." I was around ten.

When my grandmother could not say anything and had no further tears she began to sing a song, a song she sang many times when she talked about her own children who died in their childhood because of poverty. "When the little Chinese cabbage became weathered, a little girl's mother died. She was only two or three years old. The only fear she had was that her father would remarry and she would have a stepmother..." Each time when she sang the song I always forced her to tell me what she was singing though I knew it clearly. She never responded to me. I forced her to sing it loudly and I said, "What are you ashamed of? Why do you not sing it loudly so that everyone can hear?" She simply said she was singing for herself.

I remember when she cried while moving along the wall her small figure looked much smaller.

I do not know why I kept on torturing my grandmother. But I know when I heard her singing and saw her despair in her eyes, and the wrinkles on her face, I felt my heart being twisted. And I know that I felt it was evil that I treated her in such a terrible way. And I know that I felt if it had lasted a little bit longer I would kill myself.

The only punishment I gave to myself was to tell my father that I made my grandmother cry and I did it purposely. I knew he once slapped my aunt, his younger sister, when she quarreled with my grandmother. It was when she was thirty seven, a mother of two children. And I knew my father yelled at my other aunt, his elder sister, when she allowed her son to take an apple from my grandmother's room. But my father never shouted at me after I told him what I had done to my grandmother. He simply said I should not break my grandmother's heart. He said she had had too much suffering for her whole life.

And I remember each time, a few minutes after I made my grandmother cry, I always went to her room. The door was always half closed. She always lay on her bed with her eyes closed, facing toward the wall. I always walked quietly and slowly to her bed, climbed up on her bed, hugged her completely, and put my face against hers. I said, "Nanny, I was wrong. I was wrong. I promise I will never never make you cry. Please do not cry any more. Please. I will be good for you for my whole life. Please do not cry. Please talk to me. I will never drive you out. I cannot live without you. I want you to be with me. Please do not be angry with me. I was wrong." My grandmother would open her eyes slowly, with tears coming out again. She murmured, "I have no home. I have nowhere to go. I only have one granddaughter and it is you. How could you let me leave? How I can leave you?" She then turned to me. Her face was full of tears. I tried to use my hands to wipe her tears. She suddenly hugged me tightly. "I have nowhere to go and I do not want to leave you. This is my home," she said, softly but clearly.

The last time I said terrible things to her was just a few days before she died. She took my cousin to see my rabbit and she opened the case to let her touch it. I said to her firmly, "You are so close to her so let her take you to her place. You are not welcome by the family here. Go away!" Her face was suddenly frozen. I saw it but pretended I did not see it. I said to the girl, who was two years older than I, she could take the rabbit if she wanted. She said no. I said I was serious and I insisted on her having the rabbit. It was bought by my grandmother for me as a present. She paid ten yuan, a whole month's money given by my mother. My grandmother did not say anything but her face looked blue. The girl took the rabbit with her.

Then my grandmother could not get up. She refused to eat any meat, which she liked a lot. She refused to have a sip of baijiu, the Chinese wine, which she always had with dinner, and now she kept her door closed all the time.

The day when she died was Sunday, February 3, 1991. It is the day which was the arrival of spring in the Chinese lunar calendar. I went to see her in the morning as I usually did. This time she showed me her hands full of dirt. I asked her if she fell over last night. She nodded and then shook. I brought my father to my grandmother's room. He asked if she wanted to be sent to hospital. She said no, loudly and clearly. She then used her strength to get a bankbook under her pillow. She moved her lips to the corner towards me. My father asked if she meant the bankbook was for me. She nodded and her tears came down again. There was 200 yuan in the bank account and it clearly showed it was put into the bank in the amount of five yuan each time between 1982 and 1989, and the amount of ten yuan each time between 1990 and 1991. It was the amount she had saved from the money my mother gave to her.

I remember I was the only one with her when she died. She cried quietly. Two drops of tears came out and fell very fast to her neck. And she died.

北京小孩

7

北京小孩

GEESE

I had two geese when I was a child. They were from my aunt, my mother's eldest sister. I loved geese. And I always asked my aunt to give several baby geese to me. And one summer when the mother goose gave birth to the baby geese, my aunt asked me to take two. I put the two geese in a basket and took a bus. I was afraid that the conductor might stop me from getting on the bus. So I used my handkerchief to cover the top of the basket and told the baby geese to be quiet. But they were too naughty. They made a big noise just when I got on the bus. All the passengers looked at me. So did the conductor. I looked at them and stuck out my tongue and then lowered my head. The people all laughed. And the conductor said to the other passengers that he needed three seats: one for the girl, the geese mother, and the other two for the baby geese. I looked at him and laughed embarrassingly.

When I got off the bus at Xizhimen my grandmother was at the bus stop. She always waited for me at the bus stop each time when I went to my aunt's place. I showed her the geese. And I was so happy that I swung the basket to her and one of the baby geese jumped out. I was scared as I thought it might be hurt. It was scared too. It made noises and ran everywhere. My grandmother and I ran after it and all the passers-by stopped and tried to catch the goose for us. And finally my grandmother got it. I touched the baby goose. Its feathers were wet and warm. I looked in its eyes. They were full of uncertainty. I said to my grandmother, "Let's bring them home."

My grandmother built a small shelter for the baby geese. She fed them with hot corn flour mixed with green vegetables. Every day I played with the geese after school. I used a small stick to chase them to the Gaoliang River in front of my house. No matter how hard I tried, they were afraid of getting into the water. There were a few times that I threw them into the river and they always ran back to the river bank. I liked watching them swimming back to the river bank. They did it in a rush but they were so proud of themselves.

They were scared but they still raised their necks. Their red foreheads became redder and brighter when they were in the river. And my grandmother always said to me to be patient. She said they were just one month old and they were just babies. I liked waving my stick chasing the geese, walking behind them, with my grandmother walking beside me.

However a few weeks later, one of the geese suddenly died. I did not know what was wrong. It did not go out in the morning when I opened the shelter. And in the afternoon when I got home it died. Its feathers turned to white from yellow. Its head was lowered outside the plank of the shelter. Its neck was stretched. And its eyes were open. My grandmother said it moaned for the whole day and when it moaned the other goose walked around it and tried to comfort it. She said to me to bury the goose under the date tree in our garden. I dug a hole and put the handkerchief that I used when I brought them underneath the goose. When I held it, it was still warm and its feathers were getting coarse as it was growing up. It was the warmth that I had when I touched my grandmother when she died. It was the same warmth.

At night the other goose did not sleep. It kept on moaning and moaning. I went up and opened the door. When it saw me it became quiet. I said to it to go to sleep. But it came to me. I touched it. Its feathers were coarse and warm. I told it to be good and go to sleep. It did not want to leave me. Suddenly my mother came out and told me to leave the goose and go back to my room. I said I was thinking it might be better that I let it stay in my room because it might miss its friend. My mother grabbed me and shut the door. "Go and sleep," she said.

I heard the goose moaning and moaning. And then I fell asleep.

In the morning I went to the shelter but I could not find the goose. I went out of the house and looked around but still could not find it. I did not know what had happened. I ran into my grandmother's room and when I opened the door I saw the goose was sleeping on a cotton mat in the corner. And there was a mirror against the corner. And in the mirror was its own image. Its head was towards the mirror. It slept so deeply. I looked at my grandmother and she was looking at me with a smile on her face.

My mother did not allow the goose to stay in the room. She said it smelled. She insisted that the goose sleep in the shelter. So on the following day my grandmother got a baby hen, almost as old as the goose. She let the two of them stay in the shelter. The goose was a little bit afraid of its new friend. It looked at the hen, went closer to it and then ran. The hen did not make any sound but looked at the goose cautiously. I asked my grandmother what if they did not like each other. My grandmother looked at me, and then the goose and the hen, and said firmly, "They will become good friends." I still left the mirror in the corner of the shelter. For the whole night I did not sleep at all. I was worried that there might be a fight. When the dawn came I went to the shelter and I was surprised to find out they were sleeping together. The hen was on the site where the other one used to stay. The goose put its head close to the hen's head. And the hen kept its eyes half open. My grandmother came to me and touched my head. I looked at her. She was smiling.

From then on whenever I had time I always took a walk with the hen and the goose and my grandmother was always with me. I did not use any stick at all. The goose always followed the hen. And the hen always followed my grandmother and me. Sometimes I asked my grandmother to walk in an opposite direction. The hen stopped in the middle, with its head towards one side and then towards the other side. Finally it turned back to the goose and they both walked back. I laughed and my grandmother laughed.

When summer passed, both of them grew up. I never took the goose to the river and the goose never walked towards the river. The goose had such a big appetite. It could have at least two kilos of corn flour, plus some mixed vegetables. But each time it always let the hen have the food first. And the hen always had a little and then let the goose have some. Then when the goose left the hen continued to eat. They just did it in turn.

The hen had snowy-white feathers, and a tiny red forehead. The goose was much bigger, taller than the hen. It had completely pure white feathers and a red-triangle on the forehead. It always let the hen walk in its shadow. I said to my grandmother they were pals.

But the two did not stay alive too long. When October came, my mother killed both of them. She killed the hen first with a knife cutting its throat. She let the blood flow into a bowl and threw the hen aside. The

北京小孩

45

hen tried to struggle as its wings moved several times and then stopped. Its head was pointing towards the shelter.

She killed the goose as well. The goose did not make any noise when my mother killed the hen. It just stood quietly in the shelter. And when my mother tried to catch it, it made a big noise and it turned its head, trying to bite my mother. My mother then chopped at its head. And I saw one drop of tears from its eyes. Its head was still attached to the beautiful long neck. And the feathers were not pure white any more. They were pink.

I did not say anything. Neither did my grandmother. When my mother was pulling out the feathers, my grandmother said to her she wanted to get some feathers from the hen and the goose to bind them in a coin so I could play with it. My mother agreed. I never never played with the feathers bound with coin as all the feathers floated whenever my grandmother tried to tie them together.

On the following day my mother asked my grandmother to make goose and hen stew. I ate them and ate as much as I could.

8

DUMPLINGS

I suddenly wanted to get some dumplings to eat.

I do not remember at what age I started eating dumplings. But there was a picture in my mind about my grandmother making dumplings while I was sitting in my cousin's little bamboo cart. I think I was about two. My grandmother was standing in front of the kitchen counter, lined up with basins for pastry and fillings. The kitchen was small and dark so the light, actually just a single bare bulb, was lit all the time for

北京小孩

the whole day. She put me in the cart with one foot pushing it forward and backward, while she concentrated on making the dumplings. Occasionally she would talk to me while her eyes were focused on the dumplings, but she never forgot to change the speed of pushing the cart. She always started slowly and gently, then sped up and pushed the cart quickly, then slowed down and continued pushing the cart softly. I felt like I was being held in someone's arms, ready to sleep, but suddenly I was woken up and I was on a race horse and I started to move my body up and down, and then after having felt I was being thrown into the air, I was falling down to a thick but soft mattress. And I do not know why my grandmother changed the speed so dramatically but I remember each time when she sped up and pushed the cart heavily she was chopping the vegetables.

I remember the most common dumplings she made were the ones with Chinese cabbage and minced pork as fillings. Chinese cabbage had remained the main and even the only vegetables for my family and for most Chinese families in the 1980s, if I remember this clearly.

I liked the sound of her chopping the vegetables and I enjoyed watching her do the chopping. It was like the sound of hundreds of horses running on a plain, the thunders coming before the storm and the falling down of water from a hundred meters high cliff. Each time when she chopped the vegetables I always opened my eyes widely with my fists tightly closed.

But I also enjoyed her pushing the cart slowly as I knew each time when she mixed the chopped Chinese cabbage, with ginger and spring onions, minced pork, oil, salt, five spices, and cooking wine, a nice smell would spread from the process. When my grandmother made dumplings, she placed one piece of pastry in her palm, used chopsticks to pick up some fillings and put them in the middle of the round pastry, like a small pyramid, folded the pastry, clinched the middle, then used her right thumb and right index finger to put the pastry together, while her left hand was holding the pastry steady all the while. It seemed that with her fingers flying over the pastry, within one second a dumpling was finished, with two corners on each side going up and a big "belly" in the middle.

北京小孩

49

I used to fall asleep sometimes when my grandmother was making dumplings. And when I woke up for the second time, there would be a plate of cooked dumplings in front of me, with steam coming out into the whole kitchen. I remember the dumplings made by my grandmother were very very small, even much smaller than a thumb. She used a spoon to cut the dumplings in half, picked up one half, sent it close to her mouth, blew it, and smelled it, and then put it right into my mouth. "Open your mouth. Okay. Good girl, Open your mouth. Let's have the dumplings," she said to me. I then opened my mouth, waiting for her to put the dumpling into my mouth and then I would suddenly close my mouth, bite the spoon, and did not let my grandmother get the spoon out. "See how much my granddaughter likes my dumplings! She even ate the spoon," she laughed, with her head tossed up and backward. Suddenly I opened my mouth and showed my grandmother that there was nothing left in my mouth. "Oh. You have had it. You like it, don't you? You want more, don't you?" I nodded eagerly and clearly. She then picked up the other half and I was already with my mouth open.

My mother used to say that dumplings were my favorite. She said when I was only seven years old I could eat forty two dumplings.

I remember I started to learn how to make dumplings when I was around ten. I sat beside my grandmother, watching how her fingers flew lightly over the pastry. I put one piece of pastry on my palm, picked up some fillings in the middle, but I could not fold the pastry as there was too much filling. I had to put some back. I could not figure out how I could let my fingers fly no matter how many times that my grandmother showed me. I could only open and close my thumb and index fingers at the same time, like the way my mouth opens and closes when I eat dumplings.

And when I finished making a dumpling, it could not stand at all. It could only lie down, with an empty "belly" and burst corners. My grandmother always laughed, "We will have a nice soup!" I know the dumplings that I made were certain to burst when they were boiled. But the amazing thing was when my grandmother put her arms around mine, held my hands with her hands, touched my fingers with her fingers, to make dumplings with me, all the dumplings that passed through my clumsy hands were as beautiful as hers.

I remember that besides the common-shape dumplings, my grandmother also made some in the

北京小孩

50

shape of mice and pigs for me. The way she made such shapes seemed exactly the same as the one she normally made. The only difference is that she spread out the fillings in the pastry. When she made the animal shaped dumplings, there were more smiles on her face and she looked more attentively when she was making these dumplings and more satisfied after making these dumplings too. Each time after she finished making such dumplings she always held them up, looked around and then placed them with great care on the big bamboo plate. ... And I knew these were only for me.

I have tried to learn how to make such animal shaped dumplings but I have never been able to do this even today.

My grandmother has been dead since I was thirteen and I have never since had any dumplings in animal shapes.

After my grandmother died my father started making the dumplings. Like my grandmother, when he chopped vegetables he had the same pace but with more strength. His whole body was moving, starting from the wrist, up to the arm, the shoulder, the neck and the head, and down to the chest, the waist, the legs and even the feet. I remember each time when he was chopping the vegetables, our neighbors, both from the front and the back, always came to my house asking if we were going to have dumplings and my father replied with more joyful chopping and our neighbors laughed and said, "Okay, I am going to join you to make dumplings." Then there would be waves of chopping from the kitchens in the houses around my house.

51

My father's dumplings are different from my grandmother's. His are really ones made by a man - big, big and big, almost twice the size of my grandmother's. And the number of dumplings he makes is also twice the number of my grandmothers', and the amount of dumplings that I eat from his is also doubled. And I eat the just boiled dumplings instead of blowing them to make them cool. And I put the whole dumpling into my mouth instead of biting them and chewing them. My mother says the way I eat dumplings is like someone who has been hungry for ages. I am not ashamed of the way I eat dumplings as I know that my father likes watching me eat dumplings and he always says to me, "Be careful. It is hot. It is hot." And I always say, "They are so delicious. They are so delicious."

My father also likes dumplings but he has never eaten dumplings at the same time as I do. He always eats them after I have mine. I have been asking him why he does not eat with me. He always says he likes watching me eat the dumplings.

The first time that I really started making dumplings was when I was thirteen. It was the summer when my father was hospitalized at Haidian Hospital for his back problem. I remember he talked to other patients about the tasteless dumplings he had from the hospital. So I asked him what he wanted to eat. He said he did not have anything particular that he wanted to eat. I asked if he wanted to eat dumplings. I said I could make dumplings but I needed him to tell me what kind of fillings he wanted. He hesitated. "No. I do not want them," he said. "It is not true. You want them.

Definitely you want them. Tell me what kind of fillings you want. Tell me. I can make it. And I want to make the dumplings for you." He finally told me that he wanted the fillings made from fried crispy pastry, carrots, tofu, mixed with five spices and white pepper. And he told me that the pastry for the dumplings should be soft and I need to use cold water to make the pastry.

I went to the market and got everything for the fillings. When I got home, I started making the pastry in a big basin. I poured out two big bowls of flour and a half bowl of water, but found out there was too much water. So I added another bowl of flour and found there was not enough water so I added a half bowl of water. When I chopped the carrots, I found it was too hard to chop them into small pieces even when I cut them into slices. So I decided to boil the carrots. But they became too soft after being boiled. I was not sure if the boiled ones could be used as fillings. I do not have a sharp nose as my father has. I cannot tell how much oil, salt and other dressings that should be put by smelling the fillings. But my father can tell exactly what kind of dressing is missing and if the amount of each dressing is right or not by simply putting his nose close to the mixed fillings. I used to tell my father that he had a dog's nose and he always said, "Yes. My nose is big. Yours is smaller and that is why you cannot do it." And then I always touched his nose with my finger.

Since it was the first time for me to make dumpling pastry, some were too big and some were too small. It was because when I cut the dough for the pastry, I always changed my mind about the size. I said to myself

北京小孩

that it did not matter as long as I could make them in the shape of dumplings. I also had the problem to get the right amount of filling in the pastry. Sometimes there was too much filling for the pastry to be folded and sometimes the dumplings were too empty because there was too little filling. And once I started to boil the dumplings all of them burst. And the pot of dumplings turned into the pot of soup.

It was already five hours since I got home and I knew that I should be able to bring the dumplings to my father at seven that night and I needed one hour's bike ride to get to the hospital. While I was thinking hard about what I could do to cook the dumplings I saw the steamer. I then started to steam the dumplings. Because some were really big on one layer I could only put in two dumplings. And because some were too small on one layer I could put in a dozen dumplings. Anyway, I managed to cook all the dumplings.

And another problem arose - how to bring them to the hospital. I knew that I could not put all of them in the one-layer box as they would be squeezed and stick to each other. When I was searching in the kitchen I found a set of bamboo boxes which had two layers. So I put some of the dumplings into the bamboo boxes and got another three one-layer plastic boxes. It was already 7pm. When I got to the hospital the dumplings were still warm as I wrapped the boxes with several towels. But I forgot to bring vinegar as my father loves to have dumplings with vinegar. When he opened the boxes he laughed. And I laughed as well. "Four generations stay in one box." He used the Chinese saying "four generations living under one roof" to tell me the huge differences in the size of the dumplings. "Try them. See if it is okay or not." I said to him expectantly. He picked one up and swallowed it without biting or chewing.

"Do you like it?"

"Very good. Very good."

"Then have more. Eat them up." He looked at me, and said, "I cannot have them today."

"Why? You don't like them?"

"No. I like them. But I want the doctors and nurses to share them with me."

"I can make more. I can make more."

"No. Before you came they let me share their dinner and they told me that they want to have the dumplings with me tomorrow. I told them that you made the dumplings for me."

"Okay."

"Have you eaten anything?"

"No. There are some left at home. I will have them for dinner."

"Do not have dinner at home. I will take you to a restaurant nearby. The food there is nice."

I did not agree but my father insisted. Before I went home he said to me to bring the rest of the dumplings to him when I came to see him tomorrow as there might not be enough. He said he might eat some tomorrow morning. I nodded.

When I got home my mother asked me where I got the dumplings. I said I made them. She said they were even worse than pig's food. I said no. I said my father said they were nice. "Try it,'" said my mother. I picked up one, put it into my mouth, but spit it out immediately. The taste was terrible, bitter and strange. I wondered if this one was an exception so I picked another one. It was the same and not completely cooked. I then picked another one. The same, another one, still the same.

On the following morning I went to see my father. When I got there it was 7am and my father was having the dumplings. He put hot water into the dumplings. He picked one up and put it into his mouth and swallowed it. "No. Do not eat them. They are terrible." I shouted trying to stop him. He looked at me without saying anything, but picked up another one, put it into his mouth and swallowed it. "No, no." I ran to him, trying to take the dumplings away.

"They are nice. They are nice."

"It is not true. I tried them last night and it was even worse than pigs' food." I cried. "You should tell me. You should tell me."

"Listen, they are nice and I like the dumplings you made," he said to me firmly, picked up another one, put it into his mouth, swallowed it and then another, and another one.

Since then I have never offered to make any dumplings. But I am ready to make some for my father again and I will make some. And I am sure they will be good.

9

TEA AND TEA POT

I do not remember the first time that I had tea. It was green tea. And it was from my father's mug. Actually it was not a tea cup or mug. It was just a jar which was used to keep canned fruit. I remember the tea was very very bitter. I just had a sip and could not swallow it. I asked my father why he liked tea. He just looked at the big jar and laughed. He said it was nice. And I said it was too bitter.

I remember I was always curious about my father's drinking tea. I do not know how many jars of tea he had during the day. But I know that he used to have at least ten jars of tea in an evening. And when he was writing something he had more tea and the tea was even more bitter. And I remember the tea leaves were always as high as half way up the jar.

I did not like tea at that time. But I wanted to be like my father and I wanted to drink tea. I remember I once put some crystal sugar in his tea and I was so proud of myself. I told him that the tea was so nice. But when he sipped it I saw his eyebrows twist. He did not like it. But from then on he got an empty small fruit jar for me and he always made tea for me too. I do not know how he made the tea and what he put in the tea but I could tell that the tea was not bitter at all. I asked him and he said it might be because of the jar which was a sweet peach container.

I remember when I was around ten years old my father got a set of neat white china tea cups with a tea pot. When he had tea he used to move the lid of the cup to one side of the top of the cup and drink the tea with one hand. His right thumb held the bottom of the tea up and his right index and middle fingers held the lid and the edge of the cup. He sipped the tea. And then he moved his index and middle fingers to put the lid back. I was amazed by the way that he drank and I wondered when I could do this.

One day I asked him if he could make tea for me in the neat white tea cup as he was the only one that used the cup. He looked at me and nodded. Once he made the tea, I tried to reach the cup. He told me it was hot. I was too eager to drink the tea like him. I tried to hold the bottom of the cup with my thumb and tried to use my right index finger to touch the lid. Suddenly the lid flipped over and the cup flew to the other side. All the tea was spilled. The cup and the lid had fallen to the ground with a clear and sharp sound. The dark green leaves fell on the white broken pieces of the cup and the lid. I looked at my father. It was so quiet until my mother came in.

北京小孩

I knew that I made a huge mistake as my mother scolded me for being the one to make my family penniless. I cried, with tears falling down to the broken white pieces with dark green leaves and transparent water drops. I bent down to put all the pieces together. I felt I was trying to put the broken cup together. My father did not say anything.

On the following day he bought another set of tea cups and a tea pot. He said we had plenty of cups to make tea. And I noticed from then on he only used his hands to hold the cup handle when he drank tea. I did not ask him why he changed the way he held the cup.

I then started the habit to have a cup of tea in the evening. And each time it was my father who always asked me if I wanted some tea and made the tea for me if he was at home. And I always used a big empty fruit jar for my tea cup.

Years later when I was at university my father bought a pottery tea pot for me. He said to me if I used the tea pot for many years it would keep the smell of tea even when I just poured water into it.

It was the one in the shape of a tree trunk. Its body was dark brown and decorated with flowers and the neck was like a tree branch. It had a filter inside. I asked my father how I should drink the tea. He said I just drank the tea through the pot. I laughed and he laughed. Then he took out another tea pot. It looked exactly the same as the previous one but the only difference was that it was much smaller. I said to my father that I would use the small one and he should use the big one. He said they were all for me. I said no. I insisted that I keep the small one and he use the big one.

From then on my father and I hold our own tea pots, suck the tea from the mouth of the pot, and look at each other and then laugh. And each time my father always says to me that the tea is hot.

北京小孩

10

KINDERGARTEN

I do not know if all little girls have fantasies. But I know I did not or at least I do not remember.

I do not think I have ever talked to my dolls. I do not think I have ever played any games with my dolls. I do not think I have ever dreamed of being a princess.

I went to kindergarten at the age of four and a half years old, much older than most children from big cities in China. I do not know the reason that my parents

北京小孩

decided to send me to a kindergarten as it happened overnight.

It was a foggy morning. My parents took me to a park in China Meteorological Administration Bureau to see an old man playing tai-chi sword. He wore a loose white shirt and pants. He looked very serious. I remember he did not stop playing with his sword while my parents talked to him. He just glanced at me once when he finished. And my parents walked fast in small paces to follow him while talking to him. Their voices were so low that I even thought they themselves could not hear what they said. My parents had full smiles on their faces when they talked to the old man. Finally the old man nodded his head, and then left. My parents told me that the old man arranged for me to go to the kindergarten only for children whose parents worked for the Bureau.

I could not remember my first day at the kindergarten. I only remember I was asked to sit in a class with a bunch of children in the morning. In the afternoon some teachers came to us and chose some children to be their students.

I was so nervous as I saw many children being called and chosen with just a few left. I thought no one would want me. Suddenly a middle-aged woman came to me, and asked, "Do you want to be in my class?" She bent down and looked in my eyes. Her hair was not dark but gray. I could see the wrinkles around her eyes and forehead. I nodded strongly.

Her surname is Liu. And all the children in the class called her Teacher Liu.

She introduced me to all the other children. Then she brought me to the dormitory. I shared the dormitory with all the other children. It was a huge room. Each child had their own bed. There were at least fifty children in the dormitory. I do not know the exact number as I had never been able to see the other end of the dormitory.

The day I went to the kindergarten was the day that the kindergarten decided to have the parents pick up their children on every Friday instead of every day. I remember many girls cried and I did not feel sad at all. Teacher Liu praised me in front of all the others. She said I was a brave child. And she said all the teachers liked brave children.

I did not get along with the children in my class, particularly the girls. I remember one girl was the head of all the girls in my class. When the girls play-acted she was always the queen, the princess or the daughter from a rich family, and the others were her servants. They never asked me to join them and I had never been bothered to get involved with them. I do not remember how I passed the time when I was alone though I remember there were several times I looked for others who were also alone. There was always another one or two girls that were not allowed by the head girl to join in her team. These one or two girls normally drew pictures or played with the small wooden pieces to make houses. I normally asked them what they were doing even when it was clear to me what they were doing. I know I did not want to talk to these one or two girls as I did not like them but I know I wanted to show the head girl and her followers that I had my own companions.

I only cried once during my one year life in the kindergarten.

One day the head girl asked me to join them and asked me to be the princess and she was to be my servant. I did not know what I should do. It was an honor for me. I tried to say no to her as I had no reason to believe she could be so nice to me. She forced me to be the princess. She said I should not say no. She said if I said no it meant that I did not want to be friends with her and her group. I told myself they might want to be friends with me and it would always be better to have a group of people to socialize with. I agreed.

But it was not as I thought it would be. The girl, who cooked-up the plot, as my servant in the play, led all the other girls, also my servants, to rebel against me, the princess in the play. They pushed me, ran after me, tried to catch me, and ... I grabbed a chair, threw it at them, and hit the head girl. They all stopped. There was such a moment of extreme silence. The head girl turned away from me, shouting, "Su Wei bullied me. Su Wei bullied me." The other girls in her group made a noise by saying, "Get her to Teacher Liu. Get her to Teacher Liu." I grabbed another chair and held it above my head. These girls just kept on shouting. None of them made any attempt to approach me. The girls who were always left out by the head girl and her group sneered at me. They passed by me saying, "She deserves such treatment. How stupid of her to want to get involved with them!

How stupid she was to be so vain!" I let my tears come down.

When Teacher Liu came I was still holding the chair. She saw my tears. She said to me it was not too late for me to know I was wrong. She asked me to put down the chair and apologize to the head girl. I ignored her. She said it to me again. I still made no response. She said she would get my mother to take me home.

In the evening, Teacher Liu came to say goodbye to us. As before she kissed every child. She used her hands to hold the head girl's face, and hugged her. When she came to me, trying to kiss me, I turned away and ran.

When we had lunch on the following day, I had two meat balls. And I asked for another one as I always asked for more food. Teacher Liu said to another teacher loudly, "She always eats a lot." I felt I was being insulted. So I left the bowl in front of her without saying anything.

A few weeks before my first celebration of the International Children's Day, June 1st, girls from my class were to be selected to form a dancing team. I had no interest in it at all. And the head girl and her group all said I could not dance as I was deaf to rhythm, and I was stiff to dance. I did not really listen to what they said. I crossed my feet, moving them forwards and backwards. Twelve girls were selected including the head girl and her group. Teacher Liu said the next one who would be the last one was the one to lead the dance. And she said it was "Su Wei"!

I thought something was wrong with my ears. I had never danced before and I had no interest in dancing.

All the other girls suddenly began to talk, like sparrows. I said to myself since someone wanted me to lead the dance I just took it for granted. I knew before I took the offer I had made up my mind if someone said to me that I was not doing well I would leave without saying anything. And I knew I was cautious about defending myself from any gossip and any unfair treatment. I remember I learned hard and practiced hard but I never used any of my own time unless Teacher Liu asked me. I just did not get involved too much. And I was thinking of taking revenge on Teacher Liu and all the other girls. And I had an idea.

On June 1, all the children's parents, and officials from the China Meteorological Administration Bureau, Xicheng District and Beijing Municipal Government all came to see our performance. I dropped one of the scarves in my hands purposely, and then a few minutes later I let one of my shoes slip down. I wanted people to laugh and I wanted them to feel ashamed of me. I wanted them to shout at me and scold me. Nothing happened. When the dance was over, people asked us to dance again. And the officials from the first row came to the stage. They said to me I did so well that they were proud of me. And they hugged me.

So the result was I and the other girls were invited to dance for the public audience several times later.

I wondered why people were nice to me when I tried to play with them, and why people treated me badly when I needed their help.

I have never had the chance to ask anyone. I only know Teacher Liu had cancer two years before I went to middle school. And I remember she was extremely skinny when I met her in a market. And she still talked about how proud she was of me and of the dance.

北京小孩

11

HOSPITAL

My father said the first time I was hospitalized was when I was only one year old. I had an infection in my lungs. I had no memory about this.

The second time was when I was around four years old. I remember I had a bad cold and I stayed in Beijing Children's Hospital. There was a group of children staying in the same room. Among them, there was a big boy who seemed to have been there for a long time as he

北京小孩

knew every doctor and nurse there. I remember the first day when I was there he came to me asking me what kind of illness I had. I said I did not know. He then looked at the card at the foot of my bed and said to me, "Nothing serious. It is just a tiny cold." He did not have any hair on his head and his face was extremely round. He was the only one that always had a lot of jokes and stories to tell. I remember I spent most of my time listening to his jokes and story telling. And he was the first one that laughed after telling his own jokes.

Every child in the ward had their own names. They were simply called by the places where they were from. I was from Beijing so I was called Xiao Beijing. The big boy was from Shandong and he was bigger and older than the rest so he was called Da Shandong. One girl from Shannxi was called Xiao Shannxi and a boy from Henan was called Xiao Henan.

I remember every morning after the doctors inspected every child patient in the ward we started talking nonsense. Most times we talked about the dreams we had last night, our goals and wishes.

It was very strange that all the others had the same dream every night but none of us was tired of telling and listening to the same accounts day by day, week by week. Da Shandong always dreamed he was running in the corn fields, and playing hide and seek with his brothers, and he always said he wished he could go to Tian'anmen Square to see the flag raising. Xiao Henan always dreamed he was eating the noodles made by his mother, and he always wished he could have plenty of noodles to eat. Xiao Shannxi always dreamed of her lamb that was born two weeks before she was taken to Beijing, and she always wished she could have many many sheep and take them to the grass everyday. I do not remember what I said about my dream and my wish. I remember Da Shandong was twelve, Xiao Henan was nine, and Xiao Shannxi was nine. They all had pale faces and I knew that getting a cold would be very dangerous to them. Actually it was Xiao Henan that told me that three days after I stayed in the hospital.

I remember for me the one-month stay at hospital seemed extremely long. I was the only one in the ward that took different kinds of tests and analyses every few days, taking intravenous medicine and tablets. I wondered why. Xiao Shannxi said to me that it would not last more than three months. She said after three months all these would be gone and I would have my "complete freedom" except leaving the ward.

I remember I once asked nurses why children in this ward were not allowed to go out but all the other child patients could go out in the morning, in the afternoon and in the evening. The nurse, with only her eyes exposed under her white mouth mask and white hat, looked at me, and then said, "Because we like you too much and we do not want to lose you." "How could this happen?" I was puzzled and looked at her. She seemed to smile. She looked in my face and said, "You will know when you grow up."

I remember I spent the whole July in hospital and when I left it was in the middle of August. I remember Xiao Henan was so happy to know that I was to be discharged from the hospital. He said to me there were

北京小孩

several other children sharing the room with them but they were transferred to somewhere else at night and they never came back. I remember Xiao Shannxi kept on asking doctors when she could leave but all the doctors and nurses only said, "Soon, soon." Only Da Shandong was sad. And I remember on the day that I left the hospital, Da Shandong said to me that he would probably not see me again. I asked why. He said he did not think that he could see me again. And I noticed the other two were puzzled but the nurses turned their faces away from us.

北京小孩

Years later I knew at that time all the children in the ward had blood cancer. I was lucky though doctors suspected that I also had blood cancer. My father said I was lucky. And I think I was. Sometimes Da Shandong, Xiao Henan and Xiao Shannxi came to my dreams with their pale faces, telling me their dreams and their wishes. When I tried to hold their hands they all avoided me and disappeared. I think I am missing them now.

When I was thirteen I was hospitalized again. I had just finished all the exams. I remember in the morning I suddenly felt extreme pain in my stomach. It seemed like a knife was twisting my stomach. I told my mother and she said it might be okay soon so I went to school to help teachers register students' marks. But I could not sit straight. And I kept on throwing up everything in my stomach though only bitter water. The pain in my stomach was going to kill me. I told the teachers that I did not feel well and went to my mother's school as her school was on my way home. She was busy and could not look after me. I phoned my father and he came with a car.

He and my mother took me to Haidian Hospital. It was lunch time so there were no doctors there. I could not raise myself up and I could not find a position in which I could feel better. My father shouted in the corridor of the hospital. A male doctor came out. He asked us to wait for another one hour as it was the noon rest hour. My father was angry and shouted, "Do you expect my daughter to die at the hospital? I will go to talk to the president of the hospital!" The president of the hospital is one of my father's friends. The doctor reluctantly asked us to wait for half an hour as he needed to get something prepared. I do not remember what he did except he put his hand on my stomach, pushing down and asking me if it was painful or not. And he gave some tablets to my father and said, "Nothing serious. It will be fine tonight." My father doubted it.

On the way home my father asked me if I wanted to eat anything. I did not have the strength to raise my head or say anything. He asked the driver to stop at a restaurant near my mother's school, and got one roast duck for me. He said I could have it for lunch. I love roast duck and I could eat up one whole duck beside some other dishes. But that day I did not have any interest in it at all.

Once we got home, my mother went to school again and my father stayed. I remember for the whole afternoon and whole night I could not lie down at all. I kept on throwing up everything in my stomach till the

北京小孩

73

bile from my liver came. My father and my mother kept on coming to my room to see if I could wait for the morning.

When the dawn came my parents took me to the same hospital. And when the hospital was open my father took me to a doctor directly. She was his friend. The doctor asked me to undergo an analysis and when the report came back, she said, "You must be hospitalized." She asked me when the pain started. I said it was from yesterday morning. She said I was lucky. She said people who were misdiagnosed for forty eight hours would definitely die.

When my father took me to the ward he was told that he needed to pay 3,000 yuan as deposit. My father said he did not have the money now. He said he only had 1,000 yuan. He asked if they could let me be hospitalized and he would go home to get the rest of the money. But he was refused. He was furious. He slammed the door and went out. I was lying on the chair close to my mother. I just wanted to find a position to feel better. Half an hour later my father came back. The phone from the office for the wards rang. It was from the president of the hospital. He said he would guarantee that my father would pay the rest of the money. So I was hospitalized.

I remember my father fell asleep while letting his head rest on my legs when I was taking the intravenous medicine. And I heard he was snoring. I felt numb on my whole body but I did not want to move. I wanted him to sleep well. A doctor came in. She shook my father awake. "You cannot sleep here," she said. My father suddenly stood up. My mother came in and she decided to let my father go home.

For the first week my parents came to stay with me day and night by sitting along side my bed. I was the youngest patient in the hospital. Every day other patients would come to my door, asking what was wrong with me. I remember there was one patient who had some problems with his brain as he could not speak and think well. Every day he ran to my room, pushed the door, left two apples in my mother or father's hands and ran away. And if my parents tried to give him the apples back he would cry.

At that time I stayed in hospital for three weeks.

My parents still talk about it very often. They say I was lucky that I didn't die.

北京小孩

75

12

北京小孩

EYES

I remember when I was a child I used to put on my grandmother's glasses because I wanted to look knowledgeable. One of the boys from the kindergarten where I went wore glasses and teachers there liked him very much and he was regarded as the brightest one in my class. I remember I once told my mother that I wish that I could wear glasses. But she scolded me by saying I was so stupid to have such an idea and she said it was extremely ugly to wear glasses.

I do not remember at which age I found that everything on the blackboard was blurred. I think I was around eleven years old. I did not tell anyone in my family about this as I did not know what was wrong. I was lucky at that time as I was the head of my class and the head of all the students in my primary school, Xiangdong Primary School. I told teachers that I could not see the blackboard clearly and I did not know the reason. And at that time students who had high scores in their studies were arranged to sit in the middle of the classroom right at the front. So I did not really have any problems.

I remember one day my aunt, my father's elder sister, told my father that her son could not see the blackboard and they took him to hospital and the opticians said he was near-sighted. I remember my aunt said to my father that she did not understand how it could happen as she and my uncle both had good eyesight. I asked my aunt to explain to me what near-sighted meant and started to read some books about it. I found out that it was very common among all the juveniles during the time when they developed their bodies. So I said to myself that I was alright until one day I saw my cousin wearing glasses. He looked completely different. The two thick plastic pieces of lens were like two walls in front of his face. And when he sweated the glasses fell down to the tip of his nose, and he had to use a rubber elastic band to tie the glasses around his neck in case they might fall. He looked stupid, I thought. I told myself I should never wear glasses.

I hid the fact that I could not see the blackboard clearly from my parents until one day my aunt asked me if I could not see things clearly. I nodded. She talked to my father. She said to him that I might have become near-sighted as I started to squeeze my eyes to see things. My father then asked me if it was true. I said yes but also told him that sometimes if I opened my eyes hard and big enough there would be one drop of tear coming out and I could see things clearly. I said to him that I did not want to wear glasses because I did not want to look stupid. My father did not say anything.

A few days later he asked my mother to take me to a place near Xinjiekou in Xicheng District where an old woman used acupuncture to "cure" near-sightedness. She had a bunch of sharp long needles with plastic handles on one end. Normally she left them in a bowl of water. I remember there were a lot of letters hanging in her room which said she was good at curing near-sightedness. My mother took me there three times a week and each time when the old woman put the needles on my head I felt something was trying to take away my whole body. But my father told me she was good. And she was good as my mother introduced her students and the children from her colleagues to this old woman. Their eyesight was getting better and better. But I was an exception.

I do not know when my father started to buy sheep liver every day. He told me eating sheep liver boiled in plain water would help me to have better eyesight. Then I started to eat the plain boiled sheep liver. I still remember every day after dinner my father would bring a pot with the boiled sheep liver. He watched me eating

北京小孩
79

up the liver. I like all the animals' insides and I like liver but I could not bear the boiled plain liver. It had something to do with the flavor but I felt sick when I smelled it and bit it. I asked my father if I could have some salt. He said no to me firmly. "If you had salt with the liver it would not work at all," he said. I then picked up the liver without looking at it, closed my eyes, put the whole liver into my mouth and swallowed it.

"Look at you, look at you. It seems someone has owed you a lot of money. Did your father do something to be hard to you? Look at you, look at you! You do not know how expensive the liver is, do you? Look at you, look at you! Can you not appreciate what your father has been doing? Look at you, look at you! It is better that you were blind," said my mother. And tears came out of my eyes. "How dare you cry? How dare you cry? Neither of us is near-sighted. But you are. You want to wear glasses, do you? You want to look stupid, do you?" I could not hear what my mother said. The two thick plastic lenses from my cousin's glasses, the falling of his glasses to the tip of his nose and the rubber elastic band tied around his neck, all came to me. I told myself, "No. I do not want to look stupid."

Every day I had my sheep liver and I had it for a whole year, but there was not any improvement in my eyesight at all. And every week I went alone to the old woman to take the acupuncture as my mother stopped taking me there after a few weeks. After twenty minutes' bike ride to the bus station I got on the bus and forty minutes later I got off the bus, and after a fifteen-minute walk I was right there. The acupuncture was about half an hour long. And sometimes the old woman had something to do with her family so I had to go home right after I arrived. It was for a whole year.

I remember one day when we had dinner there was something very tender among all the dishes that my father cooked. I liked it very much. I asked my father what it was. He said to me "meat". I did not ask him what kind of meat it was. But I said it was very nice. My father then put the whole dish in front of me. "No. No. I do not need that much." I said. "Have all of them in your bowl," said my father. He then poured all the "meat" into my bowl. And it was really nice to have the whole plate of meat.

After dinner I was waiting for the boiled plain sheep liver but my father didn't leave the table. I then went to the kitchen and it was not there. When I came out of the kitchen, my father said to me from then on I did not need to eat the boiled plain liver. I did not know what I should say. I asked him if I did something wrong. My father said if I wanted he would cook the liver for me as he did that evening.

Just when I started middle school at Beijing Middle School Attached to Railway Institute, I found it was really hard to see anything on the blackboard and because I was too tall teachers could not let me sit in the front. So everyday I always asked people sitting behind, in front, left or right of me to borrow their notebooks. Normally I did not need to look at the blackboard as not many teachers wrote on the blackboard and some who wrote on the blackboard were used to talking at the same time.

北京小孩

81

But physics was very different. When the teacher used a projector he always said "this", "that", and "then this" when he showed how he did the calculation and how the electricity flowed. I used to go to the front corner after asking him but I felt embarrassed to do it all the time. Most times he and my classmates would not say anything.

But I was never bothered to tell my parents about any of these things till one day my father said to me that he found another acupuncture person. He said actually it was a team led by Mr. Wang Tianyun and the team was called Wang Tianyun Ear Acupuncture Team. He said there had been many reports about the effect of their treatment. He said to me actually they put a kind of special beans around the ears and they also developed some exercises. My father said to me it was going to work this time. And, he said, the place was based near Beitaipingzhuang and was just half an hour by bike.

On the following Sunday, he took me there. There were many young people taking the treatment. And they taught the exercises they developed to the newcomers individually. It took about twenty minutes to get all the main acupuncture points around both ears, and one hour to do the exercises. They checked the eyesight twice, one before the treatment and one after. And people were requested to do the exercises twice a day. My father asked me how I felt. I said I did not know but I would do whatever I could. I really did not want to wear glasses. I really did not want to look stupid.

From then on for three years I had been through the treatments. But nothing worked. My eyesight was really getting worse. And I found it was extremely difficult to borrow others' notes since what they wrote down seemed not what the teachers put on the blackboard or projectors.

When I was sixteen I told my father that I did not think any treatment would really work for me. My father did not say anything. He just looked at me and then touched my short hair again and again. "There would be a way," he said finally. In the following week he made phone calls everyday and took me or if he was busy he would ask my mother to take me to see different opticians from the top optical departments in Beijing. Every day we left at 7am and came back at 7pm. And finally after the diagnosis from an optician, aged 70, who was the head of the best optical hospital in Beijing, my father said to me that I was near-sighted and had to wear glasses. "I will get the most beautiful glasses and frames for you. I will," he said. My first two pairs of glasses had pink and light blue colored lenses, and soft pink and light golden frames. When I looked at myself in the mirror, I said to my father I was like a panda. He laughed but turned his head away.

北京小孩

13

FATHER

In my memory my father only lost his temper on me once. I do not remember how old I was at that time and what the reason was. I only remember it was a winter evening and he was extremely angry with me. We just had our dinner. He flipped the table and threw all the bowls and plates onto the floor and against the wall. I remember the flying broken white china porcelain everywhere in the room. I could not see anything else. I was hovering in a corner. I was scared. My grandmother

北京小孩

was still alive. She held me tightly. My mother was trying to calm down my father by holding him tightly. I do not remember what happened afterwards except that my father was wrapped in a big heavy thick green army winter coat, sitting on his bed. He was shaking. I remember it clearly that he was shaking and his lips were blue. I was scared. I heard my mother cry while calling my father's name. I remember my grandmother was holding me tightly while pushing me towards my father. His eyes were closed. Sweat was gathering at his forehead. My mother was trying to open his mouth to put in a handful of pills. Each time the pills fell out of his lips, down to the floor and rolled everywhere. I was scared. I thought I was going to lose him forever. I do not remember how many hours later, my father opened his eyes. He just had a quick look at me and then closed his eyes. He turned his head away from me. He was ready to give up on me. "Father, I am wrong. I know I am wrong. Please forgive me. Please forgive me."

It is the first time that my father lost his temper with me. I am always aware of the love from my father. And I am always aware of his worry about me. There have been many many times since then he said to me he did not know what kind of life I was going to have. There have been many many times since then that he just looked at me quietly and sadly. I have never asked him because I know no matter what I ask him his answer is always the same. "I cannot live with you for your whole life. I just want to make sure that you will have a happy life after I die." And each time when he says this I always feel extremely sad. I feel that I will lose him soon.

I remember when I was at middle school we had a text written by a Chinese contemporary writer. He wrote about the backside of his father when he was trying to climb over a rail fence to get some oranges so he could have them on the train. And at the end of the article he wrote his father died a few years later and he always remembered how his father climbed over the rail fence to get the oranges. And he said his eyes were full of tears. And I had my tears coming out of my eyes when I read this article. When I read this article to my father he did not wait for me to finish the reading. He left and went away. And at that time I suddenly realized he was getting old. Again I was scared that I was about to lose him.

Father has been getting older and older. I had never seen him taking any medicine until I was in senior high school. He has been hospitalized five times since I was in senior high school because of his legs, back, waist, stomach problems. He sweats more easily when he worries. And when his hands shake he cannot hold anything. When he walks he walks slowly and unevenly. It is no longer the way he walked with his head up and back straight. When he talks he has more difficulties to say words clearly, particularly when he worries. And his lips are getting bluer day by day. Each time when I see him and ask him how he is, he just says he feels he is getting older and older. He says maybe one day he would not wake up after going to sleep. "Do not say this," I always stop him. He then forces a smile on his face. "It is a fact that you have to face and I have to

北京小孩

87

北京小孩

face." He begins to dream of my grandmother and grandfather every night. My mother says she always hears my father shout in his dream, "Do not take me away. Do not." And, she says, if she asks my father what he dreams he only says "just my parents", followed by a heavy sigh.

I know he was proud of telling people that I was a reporter for *Beijing Youth Daily* working for its English newspaper. I remember there were many times that he told me how people were envious when he told them of my job and when he said to them "It was 'just' a good paid job." I know how proud he was by telling people that I went to England to do a master degree course in print journalism and got the degree and then won the scholarship to study, work and live at McGill in Montreal. There were many times that he told me in emails how envious people were when he told them that "My daughter 'just' had good luck."

I know how much he expected me to get a respected job with a high salary when I came back to Beijing. He has told me many times that he wants me to have what all the others in my age have. "You have your own house but you do not have a car. If you want I can borrow money to get a car for you." He has made a blueprint for me - with a stable income, going to work and coming home while driving a car, doing some traveling during holidays and visiting him and my mother any time during the week, just to have a nice meal together. There is nothing wrong for him to make such a plan for me. It is his dream but he has never made it.

When he was a toddler the whole family moved from Beijing to Yanggao County, Shan'xi Province, as the life was extremely hard in Beijing. My grandfather opened a restaurant there, actually a food stand, which changed to be a butcher's because people were too poor to go out to eat. But the butcher's business was still not good and my grandfather had to close the business and went back to Beijing alone. Three years later, my father, aged eleven, took his younger sister alone on the train from Shan'xi to Beijing as my grandfather got a job as a chef working at the cafeteria of China Meteorological Administration Bureau in Beijing. He carried on a huge plastic bag with pots and bowls on his back, with one hand holding his younger sister, walking through the crowds, struggling to get a space to stand on the train, and walking in the darkness to meet my grandfather living near the Bureau. And it was the year that his own mother died.

The whole family was supported by my grandfather. Every day my father could only have two steamed breads made from coarse corn. Everyday he had to walk one hour to school. He only had one pair of trainers. They were thick on each side, the front, the back, the top and the bottom - his elder sister repaired the shoes for him whenever there was a hole. They did not have any money at all.

My father could not go to middle school as he got an infection in his lung. He said because of the lack of money he got different kinds of temporary jobs as a laborer even when he knew that he had the infection in his lung. He has never told me how he survived. He only

北京小孩

北京小孩

told me that at the age of fourteen he was able to make 1.2 yuan per day by tending the sheep for the Meteorological Administration Bureau.

One year later he was able to earn 1.57 yuan per day by carrying wooden planks on his shoulder from the ground to the roof. He said he was the youngest one but he was making the same amount of money as any adult on the team. He was injured on his waist and his back hurt at that time. He then worked as a kitchen helper in a primary school cafeteria. It was the year that my grandmother, his stepmother, came to the family. He then worked as a helper at the Haidian Sports Committee, and then responsible for all the festival activities in Haidian District, then the head of the construction departments for the Haidian District Government and the Haidian Industrial and Commercial Management Bureau, and then became the director for Consumer Protection Office for the Bureau.

He always tells me that when he had his peak time in his career everyone in the whole district knew him and knew how capable he was. He also says he always remembers the hard time in his life. He says to me he wants me to have whatever good things he had and to have whatever he won't be able to have. I always ask him why he wants me to have everything and his answer is always "I am your father." And when I ask him what I could do in return, he always looks at me, thinks hard, and then says, "I just want to make sure that you will be able to have enough to eat and have a place to live after I die." And he walks away.

14

DOLLS

Since the age of four I have had my huge bed in my own room. The bed I had might be even bigger and higher than queen or king sized ones. And on my bed there were always two pillows, one for me and one for my toys, three dolls.

The first doll was made by my grandmother when I was two years old. She used hard plastics as head, cloth, sponge, cotton and even sand as the body. She drew a face on the front of the plastic head. She used dried

北京小孩

seeds as a necklace. The second one was a birthday present from my father. It was a model of a Mongolian girl who was a well-known children's hero. She looked after a group of sheep for the local government. One day when a snow storm came, she was tending the sheep miles away from the town. In order to get all the sheep back, she, a twelve year-old girl, fought against the snow storm and drove all the sheep back. But she died because of exhaustion and cold. The doll that my father gave me looks exactly the same as she, wearing a red winter dress, red hood with a white tip. Her face is extremely round and red. Her eyes are dark and big. I used to put some oil paint on her cheeks, lips and eyebrows as I wanted her to look more beautiful. I called her Longmei, the name of the real girl, and I called the one that my grandmother made for me Yatou, little girl. People used to say that I looked like both of them. But I always said Yatou was like my grandmother and Longmei was like me.

The two dolls got lost when my family moved to an apartment, six years after my grandmother died. I saw both of them in my bed in the morning when I went to lectures at my university, Beijing University of Aeronautics and Astronautics, but in the evening I could not find them. I asked my mother where they were. She said she did not know. She said I must have put them somewhere. I said no. I looked in every corner, unpacked every bag, hoping to find them. But I could not. I remember my grandmother taught me a song when I was little. It was a song that people normally sang when they could not find their things. I then began to sing:

"Longmei, Longmei, come out. Your house is catching fire. Yatou, Yatou, come out. Your house is catching fire." But I still could not find them. My mother shouted to me to stop getting things messed up. She said to me these two dolls were just junk, a bunch of cloth and fabric and they were dirty and should be thrown out. I did not say anything. But I cried.

My last doll was also a birthday present. It was my last birthday as a child. I saw it in a shop and said to my mother that I wanted it as my birthday present. It was the first and last time that I have ever asked her to get something for me. But she refused. She said I was too old to have a doll. I really liked the doll. She was very very tall, with her eyelids opening and closing when she was standing and lying down. If I patted her on the back she would make a sound. Although I did not say anything when my mother refused to get it for me, I told my grandmother about the doll. She did not say anything but touched my head with her coarse hands. She said to me, "My dear child, listen to your mother. She must have some reason otherwise she would not refuse you." I said, "I have never asked her for anything. It is my last birthday as a child. I just want a doll. I just want a doll." My grandmother could not say anything but hugged me tightly.

On the following day when I came back from school, the doll that I saw at the shop was right on my pillow. I went to my grandmother without saying anything. She just smiled. When I looked up at her, I could see her beautiful smile. But that evening my mother said clearly to my grandmother, "It is my

北京小孩

93

daughter. I do not want anyone to interfere when I am disciplining my daughter. Take the doll to anyone else." My grandmother murmured, "I know I am wrong. It is just a doll." "You used our money to get it for her pretending to be a kind person to her. What did you really want to get? What is your purpose?" It was very very quiet in the room until my father came in. He said to my grandmother that she should never get anything for me without their approval. But this time, he said, it was an exception. Then he took a roasted duck from his bag. He said it was for my birthday. And he said it was only for me. I ate the whole duck and I was so happy that my grandmother smiled while I was eating.

15

BIKE

I learned to ride a bike at the age of six. It was the time that my mother took me to my piano accordion lessons every Sunday morning at the People's Liberation Army Art School. She had to carry the heavy accordion so she took her bike. Because I could not ride, my mother had to ride very very slowly and I had to walk fast or run with her if my father did not have time to take me to the lesson.

北京小孩

My first bike was a red small sized women's bike. It was a second-hand one. But my mother did not allow me to use it to practice. She said I might break it. She asked me to use her black largest sized men's bike. She said if I could manage her bike then I could try my own bike.

It took me one week to learn to ride a bike. I practiced every noon when my mother came home. I normally practiced along the bank of the Gaoliang River which flowed in front of our house. Because it was at noon there was not much traffic so I did not need to worry about knocking anyone over or being knocked over.

One day when I was practicing, I heard car horns. I was so nervous that I forgot to push the brake of the big bike. I ran into the exposed irrigation pipes on the ground, fell onto the pipes and the bike shot out from under me and landed meters away. When I went back home my mother asked me what happened as she saw that the bike was scratched. I explained it all to her. She said I was too careless and she would not allow me to practice with her bike again. In the evening when my father was back, he asked me what happened as I had bruises on my face. I explained it to him also. After dinner he brought his big bike and my own bike. He said to me to try my own bike. I hesitated. But I was too eager to ride a bike so I rode on my bike. My father rode his bike beside me. We had a good ride. Just when we approached home, I saw several people walking side by side in front of me. I forgot to ring the bell on my bike. I then shouted, "I am coming. I am coming." My father shouted to me, "Ring the bell! Ring the bell! Push the brake! Push the brake!" I said, "Too late! Too late!" So I ran into these people. I was so lucky that one of then held my bike so I was able to stop.

I used the small red bike until I was thirteen. I always rode very fast and people were surprised how I could manage to have such speed with a small-sized bike. There were many times that some boys tried to have a race with me. But they could not surpass me or even if they could they could not keep up their speed. People say the way that I rode my bike was like I was sitting straight in a chair. And they say people in such a position can hardly ride fast.

My second bike was a new one. It was a mid-sized deep purple women's one. The day I got it was the day that my father bought me a pair of new pants, deep green patterned ones, and a new winter coat, a reversible pink goose feather coat. So on the following day I rode the new bike, wore the new pants and the new winter coat, but still my old yellow hood, and carried my old red belted schoolbag on my back. I parked the bike at my normal place and went into the classroom. Several of my classmates told me they might have seen me but they were not sure if it was me or not, though the way I rode my bike was unique and the yellow hood and the red schoolbag reminded them it might have been me.

However, the bike was stolen within one year. It was a snowy day. I was doing some studying in the classroom after class. There was another girl there who was also doing some work. When I decided to go home I found my bike, which I had parked in the place for

北京小孩

北京小孩

students, was gone. The girl, who also left the classroom a few minutes later than I, said to me that I could use her bike, a big-sized black women's bike. I said I could walk back home. She said since she lived a thirty-minute walk away she did not really need a bike. She walked with me in the snowy evening with a bright round moon in the sky. We talked about our teachers and we made fun of them. We talked about our futures - schools we wanted to go to, and we talked about food, as we were both hungry.

A few days later I got my third and last bike. It was exactly the same as the one I had before. One day later when I finished my shopping in a department store close to my house in Shuangyushu, I found a bike parked on the street exactly the same as the one that I had. Since I still had the key which was bound to the keys to my house I put the key into the key hole and the lock was undone. I was amazed. I wanted to know who stole my bike. So I locked the stolen bike and sat waiting for the "owner".

Half an hour later, a young man came to the stolen bike and unlocked it. I said to him, "Mister, is this your bike?" He looked at me puzzled. "Are you sure it is your bike?" I asked him again. "My dear elder sister, I was wrong. Please let me go. I promise I will never do it again. Please let me go, please," he started to beg me. I could not help but laugh. He then said to me, "I know you are plain-clothes police. But you look so young and I know you are different from the stupid tough guys. It was the first time for me." I said nothing but laughed. "So I can go now?" he asked. I laughed and waved my hand to let him go. "My elder sister, thank you so much. I promise that I will never do it again." He then disappeared immediately. So I got my second bike back.

But I left it to a man who always repaired my bike. He was a handicapped man. He did not have legs when he was born. And he also had heart problems since he was born. I called him Uncle Ding. He had a repair shop near Beifang Jiaotong University close to my mother's school. Each time when there was something wrong with my bike I always asked him to fix it for me. He seldom took any money as he said he enjoyed talking to me. So sometimes I bought some cakes for him as I knew he liked something sweet. This time I gave my second bike to him because I knew sometimes people would buy second-hand bikes from him. Three years later he died in his sleep. I did not know until I found his repair shop had been closed for one week. I went to his house which was in the same village I used to live, and his sisters told me he died from heart failure. I saw my bike was still in his room.

A few years later my father also bought a mountain bike for me. My mother has never allowed me to use it. She said it had more chance to be stolen and I needed to pay more for the parking fee. So it got rusted and was left at the corner of my parents' apartment. My father is thinking of giving it to someone else.

北京小孩

北京小孩

16

101

SHOWER

I do not remember when I started taking a shower. But I remember that in summer every morning my grandmother used to fill a big aluminum basin full of water from the tap. She always left the basin in the sun and in the late afternoon I took off my clothes, sat in the basin and took a bath. The basin was about four times the size of the face-washing basin. During the day my grandmother always moved the basin when the sun moved. I was amazed that the water was very very hot.

And I remember when I was sitting in the basin my grandmother used to lift the water with her two hands cupped together and then poured the water from my head to my shoulder and my back. She used to hold one of my arms with one of her hands, use the other hand to put soap on me, then cup her two hands together to lift water, and pour water from the basin onto me. And each time when she held me she always said to me I was like an eel. "Do not move. Do not move. Do not laugh. Do not laugh," she said while I was moving my body as she tickled me when she put soap on my body. "It tickled," I said. "You made me laugh." She wiped the water that had splashed to her face with her handful of soap, leaving the tip of her nose with tiny white foam. I pointed my nose to her. "Soap. You got soap," I said. She then used the back of her hand to wipe off the foam but most times I pushed her hand so she had soap all over her face. "Naughty girl." she started to tickle me and I could not help but laugh and had to beg her to stop. I stopped using the basin after she died.

Actually I remember since I went to primary school I used to go to my mother's school, Beijing No.105 Middle School, to take a shower every Friday except summer and winter vacations.

I remember every Friday the bathroom was very very crowded as most teachers could only go after class. There were closets with small boxes where people could put their clothes and benches that people could sit on while taking off or putting on their clothes. But actually most people would put clothes in a newspaper on the benches as there were not enough clothing boxes. I remember it

北京小孩

102

was very common that three or four people would share a shower. While they were waiting for the shower they normally talked about the students in their classes and the problems that they had in getting some understanding. Because of the conversation sometimes people would spend two or three hours there.

There was a big pool in the bathroom where water was supposed to be and people used to stand in the pool with water. But I did not see that any water was there and almost no one had ever gone into the pool. I remember that people said it was very dirty in the pool. I remember because the bathroom was too small, only half the size of a classroom, when people asked others to scrub their backs they had to stand on the edge of the pool but never really walked in to the pool.

I could not take a shower at the same time with my mother as when I got there it was normally 6pm and sometimes if there was not enough coal the bathroom would be closed. So when I was around eleven I started to go to a public bathroom, with several girls in my class. It was one bus stop away from my mother's school, and was divided into two parts, one for men and the other for women, which was different from the one in my mother's school. In her school Thursday was for men and Friday was for women.

We always met at one girl's place and took a bus, and got off the bus a few stops later. I remember the public bathroom used to open at 6:30pm and we normally got there at 6pm and waited in front of the door. When the door was open, like anyone else, we rushed to the window, stretching our arms, handing fifty cents for a ticket. Then we ran to the room where there were boxes to keep clothes. This room was almost ten times bigger than the one in my mother's school. We took off our clothes as fast as we could as we wanted to occupy a shower before more people came. We normally went to the showers furthest inside because each of us wanted to have our own. But there were many times that some adults came and wanted to share with us. We then turned to the other side, facing our backs to them. But we had not been successful at all since the adults always said, "You children could share one." And when they said this we had to look at each other and keep the one with the strongest flow of water for ourselves.

I remember first each of us only had a plastic bag in which to put our shampoo, soap, and comb. But since one girl had a plastic basket, all the others started to get one for themselves. I was the last one to have one as my mother did not think it was necessary for me to use a plastic basket. And she did not like the idea that I went to a public bathroom with other girls. "You just waste your time and our money," she said. I normally left home at 5:30pm and got back around 9pm. I do not remember why it took such a long time though I know that we spent a lot of time chatting and even when we finished the shower we normally walked back instead of taking a bus.

When I was in middle school near Zaojunmiao I stopped going to the public bathroom as all the girls went to different middle schools. And we lost contact. I went back to the one at my mother's school. But I went there at noon. And it was for almost six years. Actually the reason for me to keep going was that every Thursday evening my father always made some pork stew with eggs and each time he always left enough for my mother and me to have as our lunch on Friday. And I wasn't going to miss that lunch. My father always cooked rice on Friday morning to keep its fresh flavor.

I have not been to the one at my mother's school since I went to university as we moved to an apartment in Shuangyushu where we used gas to take showers. And I remember each time when the water was hot I always shouted in the bathroom. "Too hot!" Then my father in the kitchen would turn down the temperature. "Too cold," I shouted again. He then turned up the temperature. And sometimes the gas could not keep the water hot. So I shouted, "Can you check for me to see if the fire was still on?" "It is off," shouted my father in the kitchen. I then turned off the water as it was extremely cold. "Turn the water on," shouted my father. For me taking a shower was like a drama.

Two years later I had my own apartment and I could turn on the gas easily and the fire has never gone off. But almost every week I still go to my parents' place to take a shower.

I only know that I like the idea of having my father watching the temperature for me.

北京小孩

17

WELL

In my aunt's place there was a well and they used to pump water from the well. Because of the shortage of water, my aunt and her children used to store the pumped water in a big porcelain china barrel. On the top of the barrel was a huge aluminum spoon. And under the barrel was a dark colored china basin. I used to spend my summers at my aunt's place, a small village called Langgezhuang, north of Beijing.

I remember every morning when people in the family got up, my aunt's daughter-in-law was the first one that went to the well, put the dark colored china basin on the edge of the well, and pushed the iron handle. Water then came out from an iron pipe and went into the dark colored china basin. Once the basin was full she poured the water into the big barrel which was almost half way to an adult's chest. Normally she made the barrel half full and then pumped another basin of water for the family to wash their faces. She always asked my aunt and me to be the first ones, then her son, then my cousin and she was the last one. We shared the one basin of water to wash our faces.

She always got one spoon of water from the basin to rinse our face and rinse out the soap that we had used. The soap was yellowish and the brand was Dengta (Light Tower). But not every one could be given the priority to use the soap, only my aunt and me. And sometimes she, my cousin's wife, would put her hands around my hands which were full of soap, and then put her hands with the soap from me around her son's. Each time when she did this to me and to her son we all laughed at each other. Her hands were big and soft inside but very coarse outside. I liked letting her put her hands around mine and moving forwards and backwards. And when she did this to her son her son tried to get away from her with his whole body moving around like an eel. I was eleven years older than her son and eleven years younger than she.

After the whole family washed their faces with the one basin of water, my aunt spread half of the water on the floor and in the yard. My cousin's wife used to set up a fire under a huge black iron wok, at least three times bigger than the ones people use for cooking these days. She still used the aluminum spoon to get water from the barrel. Because the barrel was half full, she had to stand on her toes and bend over her body, and almost buried herself in the barrel to get the water, one spoon, two spoons, and three spoons. She then squatted in front of the cooker made of soil and brick. The huge wok was right above the cooker. Beside the huge wok was a big pile of straw.

北京小孩

She pulled a match from a match box, struck the match, and lit some straw which she put under the wok, mixed with the ashes left from before. When the fire was set up, she shook her arm to extinguish the match and then put it under the wok. She then kneeled on the ground, stretched out her head, facing sideways under the wok, and blew on the fire. Her two hands pushed against the ground to support her, and her face was raised at a forty-five degree angle towards the middle of the fire. Her hair was so long that she had to use one of her hands to hold her hair away from the fire, not only the dust. She did not wear a bra and when she kneeled and blew on the fire, her breast was bouncing inside her plain white blouse.

I once offered to help her with the fire and she agreed. I kneeled beside her, raised my head at a forty-five degree angle, like her, and blew on the fire. All the ashes were blown everywhere, into my eyes, my nose, my hair, her eyes, her nose and her hair and the wok. The ashes with tiny tiny fire fell on her dark thick ponytail and then turned into grayish shining dots. And her face was so red because of the fire. On the top of her nose the ashes left some stains which seemed like someone made some dots to highlight her round red face. She did not scold me but laughed and used her hands to move the ashes on my face. I stretched my hands to wipe the ashes on her face but left even more stains. She laughed again. I asked her why. She pointed to the water in the wok to me. I looked at the boiling water. I saw one round red smiling face with a dark thick ponytail in front of the chest and one small round face with short hair. And I used my hands to touch my face and she laughed. I looked at my hands and I saw stripes of stains. I understood why she laughed and I laughed.

For breakfast we often had some steamed bread which was cooked several days ago and heated on a drawer on the top of the wok. And we had some vegetables such as the ends of cucumber and boiled long green beans, both of which had been soaked and preserved in soy source and salt since the end of the previous year. They were kept in a small pottery jar so we could have them for the whole year even when the family could not afford to get any vegetables from the market in winter. We did not have anything to drink, normally just a bowl of boiled water from the wok. I remember the first time that at my aunt's place we had stirred eggs in boiled water to drink was when I was at middle school. The boiled water in the wok had been used for drinking and cooking for the whole day for as long as I can remember.

After breakfast, my cousin's wife started to sweep the floor and wiped the oiled wooden furniture with the rest of the water in the basin after we had washed our face. For a long time the main furniture that they had were one square table with four chairs, two double beds, two sofas with holes inside, one clothes closet and a TV. And I remember that when my family moved to the place in Shuangyushu where my parents live now we gave them an extra table to keep cutlery, a writing desk, and four green cotton sofas.

During the rest of the day my cousin's wife pumped water from the well into the basin and poured the water in the basin into the barrel till the barrel was full. She put her two hands on the handle, her whole body moved up and down in a certain rhythm. Because of summer, she sweated very easily. The sweat first appeared on her forehead, her nose, and then dropped along her face into her neck and down to her breast and then disappeared. She seldom wiped the sweat. She always shook her head. And her long dark thick hair then started to flow in the air.

Evenings were always the best time. Because they were peasants and they had their own fields, my cousin always had something to bring home for us to eat after dinner. Sometimes we moved the wok away and cooked corns skewered by iron sticks. And sometimes my cousin would bring some cherries and soak them in the basin with the water from the well. After one or two hours the cherries became cold. I remember one bite would drive all the heat away.

北京小孩

111

Normally it was my aunt, my cousin's son and me that would have the corn and cherries. . My cousin's wife always took the corn from the cobs for my aunt as all of my aunt's teeth were almost gone. And I remember my cousin and his wife normally picked the left corn from the cobs. While we were having corn or cherries, we always sat in the yard, with a round or square fan in hand, with a lot of bats coming to the yard. My aunt used to tell stories about the stars in the sky. And I would fall asleep sitting between my cousin's wife and my aunt, with a corn cob or a bowl of cherries on my knees.

The well stopped being used for more than ten years as tap water was introduced. But it was kept there and each time when I went I always tried to push the handle to get the water. No water came out. And the big barrel was still at the corner full of dust and spider webs. And the wok stopped being used for more than five years. Only the huge aluminum spoon and the basin were still used occasionally. They lay in the corner of their brick kitchen, which was built a few years ago.

My aunt died last year while I was in Montreal. I did not see her at all. And my parents told me my cousin and his wife pulled down the soil and brick place where the wok was put and threw away the wok into the garbage.

18

TELEVISION

Yesterday was the first time in ten years that I really sat down to watch a film on TV with my father.

I remember before I was five I had not heard the word TV. Every evening at 7:30 we put a small table in our garden. Everyone sat on small stools, ready for dinner. And after dinner we normally went to sleep.

I remember one of our neighbors got a TV. It was a color TV with a big flat screen. And they put it in their

北京小孩

yard so people from the whole area, Toudui Village, could go to their place to watch TV. Like many children, I was so excited and happy to find out there was something called TV and there were people in the metallic boxes, speaking, singing, dancing, and playing.

I remember for the first few days before dinner I always climbed the wall to see if the TV was in the yard and if it was turned on. Sometimes I could not sit for more than two minutes on the stool. My mother usually scolded me for leaving the table and being tempted by our neighbor's TV. But I could not help stopping to check if the TV was on. Even when I was having dinner, a bowl in hand, I could not resist the temptation of checking it out. There were several times I said to my grandmother, "Be quick, be quick. The TV is in the yard," when she was laying the table. I was sitting on the wall watching our neighbors moving their huge TV to the yard.

One day when I was sitting on the wall I saw our neighbor had turned on TV to adjust the antenna. I jumped down the wall, picked up a stool, and said to my grandmother, "I am gone. It is on. I must go now." I did not give her any time to say anything. But my mother shouted back at me. I had to come back to the table, held the bowl and stuffed everything into my mouth and then almost let the bowl fall down on the table. "I have finished. Can I go?" I asked my mother while looking at my grandmother. My grandmother did not say anything and did not look at me. My mother waved her hands impatiently, letting me go. I ran to our neighbor's place but found out I had to sit in the back or in a corner. I told my grandmother that I could not watch the program clearly as I was late.

And on the following day a long time after we had dinner our neighbors moved their TV to the yard. I had run to their place several times asking them if they were still to play TV for us. The wife looked at me surprisingly. She said to me they would definitely do it every night but she said it was too early. I could not believe that we had our dinner earlier than before. I ran to my place and heard my mother asking my grandmother why we had our dinner so early. I did not hear what my grandmother said. But I remember my mother said my grandmother was spoiling me. And she said if it happened again no one would be allowed to leave the house after dinner. "Don't you feel ashamed that your granddaughter went to another person's place to watch TV? Aren't you ashamed of this?" she said.

I remember on that evening my grandmother held my hands, carrying two stools into our neighbor's place. We sat in the front, right of the middle. I do not remember what we saw that evening. But I remember it was the first time that my grandmother went with me and we sat next to each other. We did not go home until our neighbors said to us they were going to turn off the TV. My grandmother and I were the only ones still sitting there.

On the next day, the dinner time was back to normal. And my father was at home. It was extremely quiet at the table. I did not say or ask anything. Suddenly my father said, "Are you going to watch TV again tonight?" I raised my eyes, looked at him, then

北京小孩

lowered them and buried my head. "I want to go," I stopped, waiting for my father to say something. He did not. So I continued. "People all go. And my grandmother went with me yesterday." "I am not talking about others. I am asking you," said my father. "No. Yes. No. No. I do not have to go," I said. But I was not sure if my father could hear my voice as I could not hear my own voice at all. "Go to watch the TV but do not stay up." My father then dropped his chopsticks and left his food unfinished. I was not sure what he meant.

But after dinner my grandmother held my hands, carrying two stools, and went to watch TV with me. We were a little bit late but we still managed to find a place in the middle. The program was a bit boring and there was something wrong with the TV as the image was not clear at all. I was looking around when our neighbors were trying to fix the TV. And I saw my father was sitting in the back of the crowd. I was about to tell my grandmother this but the TV started working again.

When the program was over, I looked back but could not find my father. I told my grandmother that I might have seen my father. She did not say anything but told me to watch the TV and not to think about anything else. She then held my hands. When we were ready to leave our neighbors said to us that we did not need to rush any more. They said to me, "We can leave your places for you." They did not tell me why and I did not ask. Neither did my grandmother.

A few weeks later, on one evening my father called me and my grandmother to the living room. I saw a TV was in the middle of our table. It was smaller and I remember it was fourteen inches and it was a black-and-white one. I asked my father if it was ours. He said to me that he borrowed it from someone else. He said I could watch TV at home after dinner so I did not need to rush.

And on that evening, my grandmother, my father and I were watching a war film, the same film that I watched with my father yesterday, though the version was different. My grandmother used to sit close to the TV. My father was sitting in the back. He drank a lot of tea while watching TV. And I was beside my father. From then on every day after dinner as long as my father was at home, he would turn on TV and my grandmother and I would go to watch TV. And we watched a lot of war films and police and criminal films. And I used to ask my father a lot of questions - who the good person was and who the bad person was and why the ending would be like this instead of that...

At that time I was seven.

We had this TV till I was thirteen. And by then it was the only home appliance that we had in our family. I remember that my teachers and classmates were shocked when they knew that we only had a black-and-white TV. All the others had fridges, washing machines and color TVs.

Six months after we got a color TV my grandmother died. I remember that once we had the big color TV my mother let my grandmother have the small one. But my grandmother never turned it on. And when my father asked her or asked me to ask her to watch the big one after dinner my grandmother always refused. And I did

北京小孩

117

not go to the living room to watch TV as often as I did before. Finally I stopped going at all.

After my grandmother died, my mother was about to throw out the black-and -white TV. I said I wanted to have it in my room. She did not agree. But my father said I could if I wanted. I never turned on the TV and it always sat on the middle of my table. It was thrown out when we moved to the place in Shuangyushu where my parents live now.

Years later I asked my father why he did not return the black-and-white TV. He did not give me an answer. I then asked if he bought it from the very beginning as I remember it was brand new. He simply said, "It is nice to have TV at home."

Yesterday when I was at my parents' place for dinner my father turned on TV, sitting in the back of the room with a cup of tea. And I sat beside him. We watched the same film that we did when we first had the TV. But this time I did not say anything. Neither did my father.

19

STEAMED TOMATOES

I am missing the steamed tomatoes made by my aunt. I do not remember what kind of vegetables we had in winter when I was a child except the Chinese cabbage and steamed tomatoes. I remember every family in Beijing used to line up in November to buy several hundred kilos of Chinese cabbages for winter. And I remember how my classmates at primary school were amazed when I told them that I had tomatoes for meals. Actually I had steamed tomatoes.

My aunt retired from a Beijing bakery factory when she was in her 40s because of her heart problems and high blood pressure. She used to buy piles of tomatoes in summer. She kept the empty beer bottles after her husband had drunk the beer in summer. After steaming the tomatoes, she put them into bottles and then kept them for the winter. I asked her how she could put the steamed tomatoes into the long thin bottles but she never gave me any answer. She scratched my nose and asked me if I liked them or not. "Yes. Very much," I said. "Then enjoy them," she said.

Almost every winter from December to February, she asked her husband, my uncle, to bring several bottles of steamed tomatoes to my place in Toudui Village, Haidian District. My uncle always rode his bike to our place, with one bag in the front basket and one bag in the back rack, twenty bottles in each bag. It was about two hours by bike from their place in Fengtai District. Each time when he arrived he was always sweating though he only wore a thin sweater under his coat. My grandmother and I were wearing thick cotton winter coats sitting around the oven with hot coals inside. I remember the bottles were freezing cold and it was the same for my uncle's hands. He is tall and bald though at that time he was only in his early 50s. He was prematurely retired from a state-owned printing house as he had seen some of his colleagues were laid off. I remember he got several jobs after his premature retirement. He was a watchman for different companies during the day and at night. He always ran from one place to another place and he never had had a whole day off.

I liked the job of getting the steamed tomatoes from the bottles. I liked pulling the rubber stopper from the bottle, with one hand holding the stopper and the other hand holding the bottle, stretching my arms each way. With the clear sound of "pang" the stopper was out. Then I would get a big white bowl from the closet, tilting the bottle, letting the tomatoes flow out. Sometimes I punched the bottom of the bottle. Sometimes I put chopsticks into the bottle, stirring and then letting the chopsticks stand in the middle of the bowl, and letting the juice come out. Normally there would be one or two whole pieces of tomato stuck at the neck of the bottle. I then hit the bottom of the bottle with my palm, put the bottle upright, and then suddenly turned it upside down. Then the tomato pieces would come out.

When there was nothing left in the bottle, I always raised the bottle, put it close to my mouth, and let my tongue clean the mouth of the bottle. And my grandmother always asked me if I wanted any sugar or not. "No. it is sweet enough." I then let the bottle stand on my tongue waiting for the tomato juice drops to gather, and flow down and drip onto my tongue. Sometimes once I put the bottle back, one or more drops would fall on my nose and I always tried to get them with my tongue but I never made it. "You should practice more," my grandmother laughed. I then used my finger to collect the tomato drops and put them into my grandmother's mouth. "Want sugar?" I asked. "It is too sweet." She sucked my finger with two hands holding my one finger.

I asked my aunt how much sugar she put in the steamed tomatoes and I was surprised when she said she had never put any sugar in. "But it is very sweet," I said seriously. "But you like it, don't you," she asked. "Yes, very much." She then laughed again. "I will make you more next year." "Really?" "I promise. I will ask your uncle to bring them to you every month," she said.

When I told my grandmother that my aunt would make more steamed tomatoes for me, she said to me, "My silly granddaughter, you are causing trouble to your aunt. She has no money. And if she gives you more she will have less for her own family. They need something for themselves."

There are four people in their family, my aunt, my uncle and their two children. The eldest is a girl who was at middle school and going to amateur volleyball team in her spare time and the youngest is a boy, one year older than I. My uncle was the only one who made money to support the whole family. Because the bakery factory where my aunt retired was making a loss like most of the state-owned enterprises, my aunt could not collect her pension every month. Normally the pension she collected was the one she should be able to have had six months ago, if the factory had had any money.

I remember that my aunt used to get some jobs to make some money for the family. She used to put on buttons at home for the clothes factories or stick on labels for the cigarette companies.

I do not remember when my aunt stopped giving us bottled steamed tomatoes. But I remember it was the time that my father had insisted on her not giving us any more steamed tomatoes when my uncle lost his jobs as watchman because these companies closed.

Now my aunt still makes steamed tomatoes for her own family though her daughter and her son both have jobs. And she still asks me if I want any steamed tomatoes. Each time when I say yes my father always stops me. "Why are you stopping her since she likes them,'" said my aunt. "She doesn't. You keep for yourself," said my father.

Just a few months ago my father told me that my aunt decided from next year she would not make any steamed tomatoes.

20

SUNSET

It is the time for the sun to go down. The first time I watched a sunset was when I was seven years old. My mother took me to a seaside city near Bohai Bay. It was a tour organized by her school. I do not know what I did or what I said wrong in the afternoon as she locked me in the room while she went out with her colleagues. I said to her I was wrong and asked her to take me with her. But she did not listen to me. She left.

北京小孩

I was alone. I stood on the balcony of the room. I cried but silently. Then I heard someone asking me why I was crying. It was a soft sweet voice. I looked for the voice. A fisherman boy of about nine years old was standing under the balcony. I told him my mother locked me in the room. He asked me if I wanted to go out with him. I nodded. He told me to jump over the balcony railing. I hesitated. He said to me the sand was soft and I would not get hurt. I still hesitated. He then put down his fishing pole and a bamboo basket and took off his straw hat. He stretched out his arms and held out the hat. He said to me he was going to catch me. He said I just needed to close my eyes. I looked at him. He was only wearing bluish shorts. His skin was very brown and his skin was shining in the sun. I closed my eyes, climbed on the balcony railing and jumped. I felt I was touched by something very warm and soft. And when I opened my eyes, I found out I was on his back. He said to me I was too heavy and I laughed. The balcony was not high as we stayed on the first floor.

He asked me where I was from, what my name was and what I was doing. I said to him I was from Beijing and my name was Su Wei and I was there for a holiday with my mother. He asked me why I was not with my mother. I said to him I did something wrong and made my mother angry with me. He said it was not good that a child made their parents angry and he said a good girl should not make her parents angry. I said I was a good girl but I did not know what I did that had made my mother angry. I tried to explain to him but I could not. I almost cried again.

He laughed. And when he laughed I could see his two white and huge front teeth. He told me his name but I forgot it. I only remember that he told me he lived in a fishing village close to the hotel.

He asked me if I wanted to see the sunset with him. I said yes. So we ran to the sun. He was so fast that I could not follow him. He stood and waited for me and when I was close to him he started to run again. Suddenly I felt something hurting my foot. I stopped running. He stopped also and came back to me. I raised my foot. It was a crab that was crushing my toe on my left foot. I was about to bend down to get rid of the crab. He stopped me, and said, "Don't touch it!" He bent down himself and used his thumb and index finger of his right hand to pick off the crab. I said to him to throw it in the sea. But he refused and put it into his basket. I asked him to show me the basket. He said he would show it to me later. Then he led me to the sea.

The sun was just above sea level. He told me that if we continued walking we could be close to the sun and we could touch the sun. I said it was not true. I said the sun was far away from us and if we were close to the sun we would be burned to death. He said no. He then walked towards the sun. I stayed still without moving. The sun was getting much redder and the color around the sun was getting more and more intense, almost like blood. The sun glistened in the ripples of the dark blue sea and I could see the reflection of the sunshine through the deepness of the blue water. I tried to look at myself in the water but I could not. What I could only see was the image of sun and sunshine.

北京小孩

127

He waved to me. I walked through the water towards him. And I felt that I was close to the sun. I felt that there was something that drove me to be closer to the sun. I felt there was something behind the sun and I wanted to find it out. I walked and walked ever closer towards him and the sun. He pointed at the sun without saying anything. The color was getting darker but deeper. The sun was still there but the darkness was approaching the sun. I just looked at the sun, and the sea. I wondered how I could become part of the sun.

And finally the sun disappeared.

The boy asked me if I wanted to see it again. I nodded my head. He said I could not as every day the sun went down at different places. I nodded skeptically but shook my head. I did not understand what he said but I thought I might agree with him.

He then asked me if I wanted to catch any crabs with him. He said to me after the sunset the crabs would hide themselves under rocks. He moved one rock close to us. There was a small crab there and it was terrified as it ran very fast. The boy said to me to stop the crab. I asked him what I should do. He jumped toward me and used his fingers to push on the back of the crab and then picked it up. He showed the crab to me. The water was coming down from the crab and I thought I saw the sunshine in the water. I asked him to give the crab to me. He told me to be careful. I gave him my palm and he dropped the crab onto it. The crab squeezed my fingers and I shook my hands and it fell into the water and disappeared. The boy laughed. And I saw blood coming from my finger. It was very red, like the color of the setting sun. The boy asked me if it was hurting. I said no. He said if I put my finger into the sea it would not be affected. I did and I felt the sting of pain as the water was salty.

He then asked me if I was happy. I said yes. He said to me if I was not happy I should pick up a stone and throw it into the sea. He said to me the further away I threw it away the much happier I would become.

I nodded and he laughed again. I stared at his white and huge front teeth. I said to him I liked his front teeth and wanted to touch them. He was shocked and embarrassed but he agreed. But I changed my mind. I said to him that I would not until the day I left. He asked me if we were to meet again. I said yes.

On the way back, we walked on the wet soft sand. We imprinted our feet on the sand and we looked and compared the pattern of our footprints. We laughed a lot.

Suddenly I realized it had become completely dark. I told him that I must go back. I said to him that I would meet him again tomorrow the same time at the same place, the balcony. He gave me the basket. It was a basket full of crabs. He put some seawater into it and said to me to keep it. He said he would get more when I went back to Beijing. We linked our little fingers to seal our promise.

But I have never seen him again.

On the night that I went back, my mother was extremely angry with me for going out instead of reflecting on myself. She said to me that I was a wild child and had got to know some other wild children.

北京小孩

129

She grabbed the basket and crashed it down to the floor. She stamped on the crabs and basket and then threw the basket away. I tried to stop her by crying "No". I said to her that I would never again not listen to her. I asked her to keep the crabs and the basket for me. But what I was left with was just my mother's slaps on my face and a few pieces of broken bamboo. The crabs did not bleed and I did not see any blood on the floor.

On the following day I was in my room for the whole day with the door open. My mother said to me clearly, "You won't dare to go out!" I stayed in the room and looked at the balcony for the whole day. But the boy never turned up. And finally I fell asleep.

21

SONG YALI

There is one person to whom I really wanted to make an apology. When I had the opportunity I let the opportunity disappear and when I tried to look for the opportunity again it was completely gone.

Song Yali is the most stupid student in my class at primary school, Xiangdong Primary School, according to the teachers. And it seemed true. She was never able to progress from the first to the second grade. I did not know how old she was but she was much taller than all

北京小孩

the others in the class. And because I always passed her house near Jingtusi on my way home teachers used to ask me to send a note to Song's parents. But I never got any chance to see them as Song was always the only one there.

Song always wore something with bright colors, either green or red. She had very very thick lips and a very very big mouth on her flat face covered by short brownish hair. When the teacher scolded her for giving the wrong answers to questions or not finishing her homework, she could not say anything but her nostrils moved up and down. She then cried with tears streaming along her nose and mouth. She had no friends in the class. All the students in my class thought she was disgusting and I was not the exception.

But I found Song was extremely good with crafts. She could fold paper into frogs and make kites, or make vases from tins. Sometimes when I said to her how beautifully she had done the crafts at our craft classes she always smiled with the corner of her mouth spread to the border of her face. And she seemed to feel that I was the only one in the class who appreciated her and she sometimes talked to me, though normally I only gave her back one or two simple words as an answer. But she looked as if she was quite content as she never showed any unhappiness because of my coldness. I never really treated her as a real person until one day.

It happened on the day that we had our craft class. We were asked to cut the red paper into the Chinese character "happy". I was really bad in crafts and normally the teacher would just give me a pass because I was the head of the class and I was supposed to be the best in everything. When I looked at the Chinese character that I made I felt I would never have a chance to get any score at all. I did not know what I could tell the teacher. The character was in pieces and I did not know how I could do it right.

Suddenly I saw the paper Chinese character made by Song. They looked exactly like the ones sold in the market. I asked her without any hesitation if I could use hers and she could use mine. She opened her eyes wide and stared at me. I said it to her again word by word. She seemed to feel it was too difficult to do this. I coaxed and threatened her. I said to her if she gave hers to me I would be her friend and if she refused, it would be her loss. Still she hesitated. I then begged her again to give me hers. I used the word "Please. Please" many times but nothing came of it. She just held her paper craft work tightly and looked at me.

I knew it was my last chance and if we were not in a position to reach the deal she would lose the only person in the class that she had ever talked to.

When there were two people in front of me to hand in their paper craft work I grabbed the work from her hands and stuffed mine into her hands instead. And I had an A Plus. I remember when Song was in front of the teacher, the teacher laughed looking down at her and asked Song what she was going to give in. Song looked at me and I turned away.

I do not remember what the teacher said but I remember the teacher laughed and laughed and played with the paper character pieces which were made by me.

北京小孩

133

And the paper character pieces fell down to the floor and Song was asked to pick them up. I heard the teacher use the word "stupid" again and again. And I remember Song with her nostrils moving up and down, crying with tears streaming down on her face. She tried to say something and I stared at her as I was afraid that she might tell the truth. But she did not. She opened her mouth and closed it. I then lowered down my head.

Song came back to her seat with a very red nose and her short hair seemed to have been messed up. Her face was like crumpled paper. I tried to say something to her but I did not. I was about to give back her paper character but I did not. I just looked at her sitting in her chair and wiping all the streaming tears with her hand.

Suddenly I felt awful about myself and I swore that I would be good to her from the next day on.

She did not come on the next day and she did not come at all. I heard teachers say because she was too stupid her parents decided to send her to a place where people with mental problems stayed.

One day when I passed her house I saw the door was open. I stopped and looked inside. I knocked at the door and went inside. A woman came out. She asked who I was. I asked her if she knew a girl called Song Yali. She then called the name and a little girl came from the room. The woman said to the girl, "Yali, an aunt wants to see you." I suddenly thought I was wrong and I said to her it was not the same person that I was looking for. I then left.

And I have never seen or heard from Song Yali.

22

北京小孩

RUNNING

The first time that I took part in a sports meeting was my first year at the primary school, Xiangdong Primary School, and I was given a piece of chocolate. It was the first time that I had ever had a chocolate. Actually it was not a real chocolate. It was more like a chocolate biscuit. It was as long as a thumb and as thick as a finger. I did not remember the taste. But I remember that my teacher gave me the chocolate after I did the running.

It was early in March. It was very very cold. Everyone was wearing heavy thick cotton winter coats at the sports meeting. I do not remember in which event I enrolled and who asked me to do it. It was a running event. And I remember I took off my winter coat, wearing a green nylon shirt, ready for the running. Someone asked me if I was cold or not. I said no but my red face and red nose and discontinuous words showed that I was cold. I did not win any prize after the running except the piece of chocolate, which was a comfort from my teacher.

北京小孩

136

I remember a few weeks later, a woman PE teacher came to my class and asked me to take part in the school's sports training team. At the age of seven, I had no idea what it meant. I only knew that everyday after class I needed to stay at school, stretch my legs, arms and whole body, jump in different ways, with hands behind and kneeling down, or only one foot touching the ground, or jumping upwards, and run in short distances with my speed changing. The training was for two hours every day after class. And in summer we had the training every morning from 8:30 to 11:30. Even when it rained the woman teacher still arranged programs for us - running the steps.

She was very very dark and very very fit. She was very strict with everyone and she scolded anyone who tried to be lazy. But she never scolded me. I remember that I was the only one that had never asked for any single day's leave for the whole summer. And she later asked me to take one day off.

I remember there were around twenty people in the training team from students in the first grade to the ones who were going to finish their primary school. I do not know if I liked the training or not but I know that because of the training every day I would have a big bottle of "berry juice" from my grandmother. It was made from a big plastic bag of crystal sugar with berry flavor. Because we did not have a fridge she normally boiled some water, mixed a half bowl of the berry flavored sugar with a tiny bit of water into a bottle, then she let the boiled water become cool, and poured the boiled water into the bottle, tightened the lid and left the bottle in a sink with water from the tap. For me there was nothing that could be more enjoyable than drinking up the bottle of "berry juice" when I was covered with sweat after the training was over.

北京小孩

137

And the other reason that I liked the training was I made friends with a girl who was four years older than me. She taught me how to play chess by using stones, how to play the game of "House Building" with a piece of chalk on the ground, and she was the first one that bought the first real ice cream for me. It was the first time that I had something made from sugar, ice and milk powder, although the one she bought for me can never be compared with any ice cream in the market today. She lived near Sidaokou, which was in the direction opposite to mine. But I always walked with her to her place as I knew that she would buy an ice cream for me. But I did not see her any more after summer. I asked the PE teacher about her. I remember the teacher said she was transferred to another school and lived with her aunt as her parents who were divorced refused to take care of her. I was sad not only because of her experience but also because of the ice cream she used to buy for me.

北京小孩

138

I did not stay in the training team long as my father strongly opposed the idea that I took the sports training for running. I remember he told me and the PE teacher that such training would take away my time from my academic study. He said he did not want me to become a runner as he did not think that I was good at running and he said, even if I could be a professional, the chance for me to become a world champion was zero and even the chance for me to take part in world champion competition was almost zero. He said to the PE teacher, "The Chinese will never be able to compete with the westerners in running. I do not want my daughter to waste her time and end up being a person with strong arms and legs but empty mind. And I do not want to see her leading a life with all kinds of diseases and wounds because of the training." He forced the PE teacher to let me leave the training.

Because of the half year's training, I was the one that always ran fastest in my class.

I remember for a long time that all the PE teachers did not like me - they did not look at me or talk to me. And I remember three years later a new PE teacher came to the primary school, as a graduate from Beijing PE Normal University. He selected me to represent the primary school to attend a district running competition. Before I said anything other PE teachers stopped him by saying, "Her father will not allow her to do this. He thinks it will interfere with her academic study." I remember the young man still decided that I should take an intensive training. But a few days later both of my parents refused to let me take the training.

When I was at middle school, Beijing Middle School Attached to Railway Institute, I was still one of those running fast in 200m and 400m. But there was another girl in the same grade who was always the second prize winner for Haidian District. She was from the same primary school. We started taking the running training at the same time but I left while she did not. At the first sports event at the middle school, she ran faster than I. From then on, she was the fastest runner in my grade in 200m and 400m. I was no longer to be the fastest one.

But I remember that each time at the school's sports meeting, my teacher always asked me to enroll in the same events as the girl did. And each time there were always plenty of milk chocolates in my seat when I came back and was defeated by the girl.

And I remember I always cried when I came back to my seat. I was too eager to tell people that I was the fastest runner but I knew that I would never have the chance.

Before I went to university I practiced the 800m running as it was part of the PE exams for entering university. I bought two sand bags of five kilos each. I tied them around my ankles. I walked with the sand bags, I rode my bike with the sand bags and I ran with the sand bags. I remember other students in my school who also bought the sand bags only used them at PE lessons.

北京小孩

I remember they asked me why I wore them all the time. I said it was cool. And it was really cool when I took them off during the PE exam for entering university. I felt I was flying. I felt I was the only one with wings. I was the first one finishing the first 300 meters and I heard that someone said "55 seconds" and I was still the first one finishing the second 300 meters and I heard someone say "2 minutes 10 seconds" and I was the first one to arrive and I heard someone say "2 minutes 55 seconds". I gave them my number and left.

北京小孩

When I became a freshman at Beijing University of Aeronautics and Astronautics, I enrolled for the 200m and 400m for the sports events for all the freshmen in my department. And I was the first one for both. I remember that my classmates said to me that they could not believe that I could run so fast. I said "thanks". I know that there was something in my heart which pushed me to take the two events to run. I know that I was certain to be the fastest runner.

One month later, it was the sports meeting for all the freshmen at the university. I did not want to enroll for any event. And I said no to anyone from the department who came to me asking me to represent the department. I thought that I almost succeeded in not taking part in the event until my father said to me that I should take part in the sports meeting when I told him that the department asked me to run for them. He said I needed to support the department. He said I should have a sense of responsibility. So I told the department that I would take part in the two events. And there was another girl who was almost half way in front of me.

And no matter how hard I tried I could not shorten the distance. I knew I was defeated again. Later when the competition was over, people said to me I was the fastest. I said thanks to them and thanked for showing their sympathy to me. I said to them I knew where I was. They were surprised but did not say anything except the girl was a professional athlete who was doing her undergraduate course at the university. I understood why they said this and I felt they expected me to accept the fact that I was the fastest if I did not think about the girl. But I could not.

北京小孩

141

From then on I refuse to take part in any sports meeting. And each time when people ask me if I do any sports I always say no.

23

RIVER

There was a river in front of the house where I spent all my years as a child and a teenager. It is called Gaoliang River.

The river was clear when I was a child. I could drink the water from the river though my mother did not allow me to do this. But my grandmother said to me it was alright to drink the water from the river.

In summer while my grandmother was getting the plants from the river for the chickens we kept, or she was washing clothes on the riverside, I either picked up stones to throw into the river or just sat on a piece of small rock on the riverside watching and catching the tiny fish and shrimps. There were several times I almost fell into the river and my grandmother grabbed my arms or legs. She was tiny but she was strong. And each time when my mother knew that I played along the river she always scolded me and forbade me from going out for a couple of days. My grandmother tried to explain to my mother that it was not very dangerous but she was stopped by my mother when my mother said she was disciplining her own daughter.

The first time that I stopped playing along the river was when my grandmother brought me to the river and told me that I could do some washing there. She said I was a grown-up girl. I remember it was the time when the sun came out. I did not know what I was going to wash. I had a handkerchief in my pocket so I washed it in the river. I just put it into the river while my grandmother was using a stick to hammer the clothes. I suddenly felt she looked even much smaller than she was. And I felt that I would lose her soon. Then I suddenly cried. I was around nine years old.

I asked my grandmother what if I let the handkerchief float in the river. She said there would be another girl at the end of river to pick it up and keep it for ever. I then left the handkerchief in the river and watched it disappear.

In the evening after dinner, my grandmother usually carried a small folded chair with her to the river bank. Normally I just sat on my grandmother's lap. She then told me the stories about her and my father when they were young and about me when I was a baby. She had been telling me these stories many many times. When I got impatient by listening to the same stories she would stand up and pick up some grasses to make a rabbit for me. I asked her to show me how to make the rabbit but I never really learned it.

Around this time the lady who sold ice cream from her tricycle was coming. My grandmother would always search her pockets to get ten cents. I then held the money tightly and asked for two ice popsicles with lemon flavor. One was for my grandmother and the other for me. I could let the ice popsicle melt in my mouth. I always swallowed it in one minute while my grandmother was still holding hers intact. I knew she would never eat it as she always kept it for me. I did not want to take it from her as I knew that most times she only had five yuan to spend. So each time the ice popsicle melted and I drank half of the melted one and left the rest in the package for my grandmother.

Four years later my grandmother died.

The river was getting dirty. People did not take walks along the river in the summer. Migrant workers stayed on the river bank. Police went there more frequently.

When I went to university my family moved out as the government wanted to expand the road in front of our house.

A few weeks before I went to England I went to the river again. Construction was going on there all the time. One of my aunts who used to live there but one row

北京小孩

145

behind us was still living there. But the house is not the one that they had. It is just a small room for her and her husband.

These days I pass one end of the river on the way to the subway. I have tried to look at the river but I know that I do not really want to be close to the river.

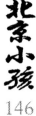

24

RAIN

I used to like rain. I liked to see the heavy rains pouring down from the sky down to the ground. For me it was so significant and wonderful to see the rain, like the waterfalls, suddenly cascading onto the windows, the doors and the buildings. I loved to hear the rains hitting the windows. For me it was the most beautiful music with such a strong sense of rhythm.

I liked to hear the thunder. I liked to see the lightening flash. I used to wonder why the thunder and flash always turned up together. My grandmother used to tell me the thunder was a dragon and the flash was the dragon's skin. Many times I did see the thunder appear in the sky as a dragon coming over.

Most times the heavy rains came with strong winds. I remember that I had so much fun by holding an umbrella walking in heavy rains against the winds. I liked my umbrella being blown inside out. And I liked seeing others having their umbrellas being blown inside out too.

I remember one day when I was sitting on the back of my father's bike after he took me to see a movie at Beijing Exhibition Museum, the rain suddenly came with strong winds. The willows were all bent in the wind. I opened an umbrella. I tried to hold it for my father. But just when I opened the umbrella I was blown down by the strong wind to the ground with my umbrella still open. I was like a pilot parachuting. My father did not notice that I fell down to the ground until someone shouted to him, "Your child is blown to the ground. How can you dare to run?" Then my father turned back. He parked his bike and put me on the front of his bike. He then held my face, examined my face and then sighed, "Did you get hurt?" I shook my head. Later in the day, my father bought some cakes for me.

And the most interesting and exciting thing about heavy rain with strong winds was to pick up dates from the date tree in our garden. My mother did not allow me to use a stick to get the dates to fall down to the ground even when the dates were ripe to eat. So I only ate the dates fallen to the ground if they were too mature or dropped by some birds. But when there was heavy rain with winds dates whether they were over-mature, matured or raw would all be blown down to the ground. Once the rain stopped I always rushed to the garden to pick up the dates. I did not have any baskets or bags with me as I seemed to have no time to think at all. I ate the dates while I was picking them up. I was so greedy that I did not allow myself to really taste the dates before I put even more into my mouth. I knew my mother would definitely tell me that she needed to give some of the dates to her colleagues and students. And each time I always felt there was nothing really left for me.

北京小孩

149

I also liked the small thin rains. But it was mainly because I liked to walk in the rain, raise my head, let the rain fall on my eyes and fall into my mouth, and then taste it with the tip of my tongue, and then swallow it. Sometimes the rain was very very cold and I could not help shaking my shoulder when the rain was in my stomach. I liked to walk in the small instant rivers on the ground which were actually a cluster of rainwater. I always tried to walk into the "river" while wearing my sandals first, and then took off my shoes and jumped and walked into the "river" with bare feet.

And I liked to fold a paper boat, put it on the cluster of rainwater and let it go wherever it wanted to go. Normally the paper boat turned aside. And I would make another, another one till I saw the boat was floating somewhere.

I always wanted to have a pink umbrella with the pattern of pieces of broken flowers. I saw that girls from my neighbors and from my class all had colorful umbrellas. And when it rained they all opened their beautiful umbrellas. I would never forget the scene of a line of colorful umbrellas like rainbows as they walked along the streets. And I was ashamed of my umbrella, an old and black one.

My grandmother had a big old-style bluish water-proof cloth umbrella with an orange handle. It could not be folded as small as the umbrellas today. Even when it was closed, it was as high as me when I was six years old. My grandmother used to open the umbrella and took me to the grocery story in the village, Toudui Village, to get some candies. I liked walking under such an old umbrella with my grandmother. It was she that normally held the handle but I always put my hands on the top of my grandmother's. I also tried to let my grandmother be under the umbrella completely but each time my grandmother put her arms around me tightly when I tried to move a little to the outside of the umbrella. I tried to let my grandmother keep dry. But I never made it.

However things changed. My grandmother died. I was warned by my mother that I was too old to play in the rain. My father finally got several beautifully patterned umbrellas but he could not find a pink umbrella with pieces of broken flowers. My grandmother's big old-styled bluish water-proof cloth umbrella has been missing. And we moved to an apartment building in Shuangyushu and the date tree was pulled out by the government. And I started to treat rain as a nuisance of life.

Now I hate rains.

北京小孩

25

151

PORK STEW

The calendar said today was the day that autumn started. The most popular saying in Beijing is that today people should eat a lot of meat because in summer people only like something light and are supposed to lose weight.

I did not know this until I was around ten years old. I remember one evening at dinner my father brought a big plate of pork stew to the table. I asked him if there was anything special for that day. He said to me, "Today

北京小孩

is liqiu, autumn arrival day. And we need to put on some weight. So we will eat more meat." I do not remember if I said something else. But I remember that my father picked up a big piece of pork, dark red and oily. It was not lean at all. Only a tiny part of the whole piece was lean, followed by the transparent fat and then a thin layer of lean meat, and then it was the thick red skin. It was so amazing that the whole square-shaped piece was like a crystal diamond in white and red, hanging from a rock which was the oily skin. Putting it into my mouth, the flavor of soy sauce, brown sugar, cinnamon stick, ginger, garlic all got spread in my mouth. My teeth first touched the skin, chewy, but the feeling was good, then the teeth went down to the mixture of fat and lean meat, soft, slippery but a nice texture, then it came across the pure lean meat, which made me feel that I was having the real meat. Then the whole piece of meat fell from the teeth to go through the throat to the stomach. I could not resist the temptation to pick up another piece. I do not remember how many pieces that I had for that particular day but I remember that the whole bowl of pork stew was empty but I was still dipping my chopsticks into the sauce left in the bowl and started to bite the ginger and garlic and suck the cinnamon stick. For me it was one of the most delicious dinners that I had ever had.

I still do not know how I could enjoy the pork, the fat pork, that much. I do not know how my father could cook the pork stew with such a wonderful flavor.

I remember that my father seldom bought pure lean pork. He said to me that the pure lean pork was tasteless and too chewy to make pork stew. And he always liked to get the pork piece with heavy skin. He said to me the skin was good for my skin. I had spots on my face and still have the marks left.

He always used a huge knife to cut the pork piece into long slices, and then cut the long slices into cubes, two centimeters on each side. Then he would boil water in a big steamer, threw ginger, garlic, spring onions and cinnamon stick into the water. When the water was boiling he put all the pork cubes into the steamer. The steam spread in the kitchen and a strange smell came out from the steamer. He had a big spoon with holes to stir the pork cubes, gently and slowly and then strongly and fast. Then the foam came to the top, he smelled it with a deep breath, then removed the steamer and got the pork cubes out of the steamer and let them dry in a big basin. He then put a wok on the cooker, added some oil, whole pieces of ginger and garlic and long spring onions. When the oil was hot, he threw the cinnamon sticks into the wok, stir fried them with a huge spatula, twice the size of the normal ones in the market. Then the whole kitchen was full of the fragrance of all the mixed dressings. With a sound of water being splashed by a stone, he threw all the pork cubes from the basin into the wok. With several quick stirs, he poured soy sauce, cooking wine, and spread some red pepper and a handful of brown sugar on each piece of pork cube, and then poured in the hot water just covering the pork cubes.

Then he would leave the kitchen, make himself a cup of tea, and watch TV. Around half an hour later, the

北京小孩

153

smell of the pork stew came to every room. He stood up, walking directly but slowly to the kitchen. The steam and smell from the pork stew were everywhere in the kitchen. There was not too much liquid left though it was still bubbling. My father then lifted the wok with one wrist, shook the wok up and down, letting each piece of pork cube get all the sauce. He then turned down the cooker. The bubbles in the liquid in the wok were still coming out continuously with tiny tight foam around the pork cubes. This time he did not go away. He just stood beside the cooker, looked at the pork cubes and breathed deeply. When the liquid in the wok became thicker and thicker, my father stirred the pork cubes again, then lifted the wok and poured them into a big bowl and then turned off the gas cooker.

There were always several pieces of skin sticking to the wok, and I was the only one that would use a spoon to get the extra meat. My father then looked at me with great satisfaction, asking me how the pork stew tasted. "Good. They are good." I scraped off the meat left in the wok and on the edge of the wok, and answered him without looking at him. For me a feast was coming soon.

I remember each time when I told people that I liked pork stew, they all laughed. They said only the least ambitious and poorest people would say they like pork stew. I was not and am not one of these people but I like the pork stew, no matter how fat it is.

26

PIANO ACCORDION

Whenever people ask me if I play any musical instruments my answer is always no.

Actually it is not true. I spent six years learning how to play piano accordion and I got a certificate from Beijing Piano Accordion School which says I can play it at the medium level. And my teacher was one of the best piano accordion players in China. But I am ashamed to tell people that I can play it as I really do not like it at all. And I almost cannot play it at all because I have never touched it since I got the certificate.

I remember just a few days after I started primary school at Xiangdong Primary School my mother told me that she had enrolled me in an accordion class and she was going to take me to the class that evening. I had no idea what an accordion was about. I just looked at her. She continued to say that piano accordion would be the only musical instrument that I could learn. She said to me that I could not learn how to play violin because if I could not play it well I would make the music sound like a chicken screaming with its neck being held. And she said to me that I could not learn how to play piano because my fingers were too short.

That evening my mother took me to the People's Liberation Army Art School for the accordion class. There were so many people in the classroom and I was scared to see that almost all of these people, much older than I, were playing accordions. I remember there was a fat young man playing some music pieces one after the other. He sat there, like an arrogant cock, pushing the reed open and closed, with his head moving up and down, left and right, and his left foot hitting the floor in a measured pace. I looked at the people around me. They seemed to know each other - they talked to each other and they laughed. All of them had accordions on their laps. But I had nothing except a popsicle that my mother got for me on the way to the class.

I was nervous. I was scared. I felt I was stupid. I wanted to do something but I did not know what I could do. I looked for my mother and wanted to say something to her but I could not find her. Suddenly I heard someone say, "It melted! It dropped on your skirt." I did not realize what it was about until that person pushed me. My popsicle had melted and dropped onto my skirt and I was left with only the stick in my hand. I was too embarrassed to say anything. Suddenly my mother came and scolded me for being a slob. She said I made her lose face. My fingers were sticky. I tried to clean my fingers by wiping them around my skirt. My mother scolded me to stop doing it. She said she could not understand why I did not think it was nasty. I felt my tears coming down. I felt I was like someone standing in public without wearing anything. I was ready to dig a hole in the classroom and get into the hole.

"You are here too," a woman said to me. I raised my head and saw that a woman was right in front of me. And a boy was having his popsicle beside her. The boy was my classmate in primary school and the woman was his mother. She asked me what had happened. I said my hands were dirty, I did not have an accordion and I did not know how to play it. She laughed and so did the other people around her. "You will know once you start you class. You can wash your hands in the toilet. There is a toilet outside. We do not have an accordion either. The teacher will lend one to us," she said, touching my head with her hands.

Later I heard my name called by a middle-aged man, wearing a grass-green army uniform. He said to me he was my teacher and his name was Shan Yuanchang. He took me to another room and another six children at my age were already there, including the boy from my class.

The teacher lent me an accordion with forty eight keys. I was not thrilled by having the accordion at all. But I do not know the reason. A few months later, before the teacher went to an accordion factory, my parents gave him the money to buy a bigger one, the one with ninety six keys. I remember there was a girl in the accordion class using an accordion that was red and white. So I asked the teacher if he could get a red and white one for me instead of black and white. He agreed. But my mother said to him that he could just get the black and white one as I would not play it well no matter what kind of color the accordion was. So the teacher got a black and white one for me. I was disappointed.

Just one year before I got my certificate as a mid-lever player, my parents spent around 1,500 yuan to get the biggest one, with 120 keys, for me, which is for the professional accordion players. I remember my mother said to me clearly several times that she and my father had used up all their savings to get it for me. At that time my mother's monthly salary was seventy six yuan and it was almost the same amount of money that my father earned. And we only had a small black and white TV as the only electronic appliance in my family, although most families had a color TV, a washing machine and a fridge with a freezer.

From then on, every week I went to my accordion class with my mother. It was a two-hour session. For me I always wished the time could be much shorter. It seemed that I was the worst one in the class. I always made a lot of mistakes when I played. And I felt that I was the cause of laughter for all the others in my class. For me it was really humiliating to be told by the teacher that I made mistakes or I could not play as fluently as the others. And each time after the class I knew that my mother would scold me for losing face. And I knew that she would punish me by saying she would never take me to the class any more and she would sell the accordion. And I knew I would always cry and beg her not to do this. And I knew she would not really do it and I knew that I really wished that she would sell it and I would never have to go to the accordion class any more.

I remember everyday, seven days a week, fifty-two weeks a year, there was not any single time that I was not crying when I practiced the accordion. And it was for the whole six years. I remember there were many many times that my mother used a stick to rap my fingers, used her palm to slap my face, and kicked the chair on which I was sitting and I fell to the ground. And there were many many times when I fell to the ground that the accordion crashed onto my chest. She said to me, "Get up. Do not pretend to be dead." And I always got up with my eyes full of tears streaming down. "Cry? What else can you do?" she yelled at me. "Can you not find anything else to do? Am I doing something wrong to you? How dare you cry while playing it so badly? You have made me lose face." She never stopped. And I knew that my neighbors were going to say that I caused my mother to lose her temper. And I knew that my neighbors were all aware that each time when I started to play the accordion there would be my mother's shouting and my crying following.

I really hated myself. I was lazy and I did not have any interest in it. I could not play it well no matter how hard I tried. I did try to practice for two hours a day for the first two years but later I found out no matter how long I practiced I was always the last one in my class. I started to lie to my mother and my teacher. I said to them that I practiced very often at home which was not true. I did not want to touch the accordion unless my mother was asking me to practice while she was standing in front of me. I did not understand why I was tone-deaf as I could not notice that I pushed the wrong key. I did not understand why I could not really enjoy it. And I started to pray that the teacher was ill so that there were no classes.

I remember there were many times, whenever we had visitors to the family, that my mother asked me to play piano accordion for them, and most of the time it was when they were having their meal. I do not know if any of them really listened to me playing the accordion. I only remember each time when I finished no one said anything except "This dish was good" or "That one is not bad." I was very very sad. I felt I was like someone in the old China making a living by playing a musical instrument in a public place to entertain people when they were eating and drinking.

My mother always said and still says that because I learned accordion I had to sit for a long time which had enabled me to sit down and do my academic study for a long time without thinking of going out to play all the time. She also said and still says because I could play piano accordion by using my left and right hands the two sides of my brain were being developed. I was not sure if any of these were true or not. I only know that now I am the kind of person that enjoys being alone.

I do not think that I have ever had any happiness by learning the accordion though my mother said to me that the reason for me to learn it was that I could have it as my companion since I was the only child in my family.

北京小孩

167

I do not know how much pleasure I had obtained during the six years of accordion learning. But there was something that would always make me smile each time when I thought about the six years.

The teacher's wife was the first one that said I was pretty. It was the first time that the teacher took me and others for a stage performance. His wife was the one that put makeup on us. I remember she spent a much longer time on me, and after the performance my teacher said to me that his wife thought I was a pretty girl. I did not want to wash my face. I remember, from then on, each time when we went out for a stage performance, his wife always spent a much longer time putting makeup on me and she always asked me to look at myself in the mirror. She used to say to me, "You are pretty."

I also remember that when my teacher was busy his son used to give classes to us and he volunteered to give extra classes to me. He said to me many many times that I was a good player. But I did not believe him at all. I knew that I was the worst one in the class. But it was very strange that when he gave us the class I did not make any mistakes. And I went into the second round of the national piano accordion competition when he was giving classes to us and actually gave me extra classes. When it was the time that he was going to have his own student I thought he would definitely choose me to be his student. But he did not. He chose the boy who was my classmate. I was disappointed.

北京小孩

Another thing that made me happy during my six years was that during the last four years every Monday evening after the class my father would meet me and my mother outside the classroom. On the way home he would stop at a tricycle stand near Weigongcun to buy a pancake for me. And it was always the same stand where he got the pancake for me. The man who sold the pancake was from the neighborhood where we lived. He always poured two spoons of liquid pastry, made from wheat and green bean flour, one spoon more than others, onto a small pan. Then he would always put two big eggs on the top of the pastry, though he only charged for the pancake with one egg. Then when the pastry turned to a golden color, he turned the pancake on the other side, spread chili sauce, hoisin sauce, black bean sauce and sesame sauce, spring onions, spinach, and then pick a big fried crispy pastry to put on top of all the sauces, used a spoon to fold the pancake with the fried crispy pastry, and then wrapped it with brownish paper. He passed it to me while my father was passing the money to him.

I always held the pancake up to my father, asked him to have a big bite first. But he always said to me that he did not like it and asked me to eat it up when it was hot. "Is it good?" he asked. I nodded and put the pancake back close to him. "Try it to see if it is really good," I said. "No, I do not like it." He pushed it back to me. I did not want to argue with him as I could not resist the temptation to eat it. My mouth was full of the smell of pancake. And when I was eating it my father always asked me to be careful with the wrapping paper. "Do not eat the paper. Do not eat the paper," he said and laughed. "Get another one," he said to the pancake man. "No. I have had enough," I said. While the pancake man had already made one for me as I was having my first. He knew that my father would always get a second one for me.

27

北京小孩

171

PERIOD

I was eleven when I first had my period. I did not know what happened so I asked my mother. She did not tell me anything except she gave me a wad of toilet paper and asked me to put it into my pants. I asked her why I was bleeding. She said the term that I should use was "daomei" (bad luck). I do not remember what else she said to me.

I remember my aunt noticed I put a wad of toilet paper into my pants when I was in the toilet. She asked

北京小孩

me what happened. I said to her I was bleeding underneath. She asked how long it had lasted. I said it was the first time and I did not know why. She said to me it meant I was growing up to be a woman and it was something that every girl and woman all had once every month.

Later in the day my grandmother came to my room with several new underpants, several wide cotton belts, and a roll of wide pink toilet paper. she said to me each time when I had my "period" (she used the term period when I used the term bad luck) I needed to wear the red pants and put the clean and soft toilet paper into the belt and tie the belt around my waist. She reminded me that I should always remember to change the toilet paper very often.

There was one time I had my period when I was at school. I did not know it arrived until the class was over and I stood up. I wore a pair of white pants. I looked at the chair unconsciously and found the stains on my chair. I used my hand to wipe out the stain and found out it was blood. I was embarrassed and was in a panic. I felt everyone must have known this. I then chose to sit on my chair, waiting for everyone to leave. Some of my classmates came to me, asking me why I sat there and wasn't going home. I lied to them that I was waiting for the teacher. I left when everyone left. When I came home I saw my mother. I said to her that I had my period and I had stained my chair. She said it was very embarrassing. She said it was not something I should spread. She said I should be ashamed of this. I felt so bad about myself and I hated that I had my period. And I cried.

Later my grandmother came to my room. She brought a bottle of white powder. She said the white powder could get rid of the blood. She said she used it before when she saw the blood on my bed sheet. She said to me to take off the stained pants and change to a clean dark one. She said if I wore a dark one no one could see if I had any stains or not. In the evening she came to me with a piece of cotton mat. She said I could put it underneath when I was sleeping so I did not need to worry about getting the bed sheet stained at all.

北京小孩

From then on, every month when it was time for me to have my period I was cautious about my pants, chairs and anywhere I sat. I always checked to look at the place I sat in case I left any stains. I always wore black trousers when I had my period as I was afraid I might get them stained and be laughed at by others. And I stopped wearing anything in light color any time.

That summer my mother sent me to learn swimming in the Children's Activity Center near Xizhimen. My period came again. I had no idea what I could do. My mother said I could put some cotton cloth in the belt, wear the red underpants, and then the swimming suit. I asked her if it was safe so that the blood would not get into the water. She said I worried too much. But I did not worry too much.

When I was at the swimming lesson, the blood went through the cotton cloth, the belt, the pants and the swimming suit. It spread in the blue clear water. People looked at me and I looked at myself. Suddenly I jumped to the edge of the pool, ran to the changing room, pulled on my dress, and ran all the way back home. I cried. My mother was shocked. She asked me why I left so early. I said everyone knew I had my period. She said to me I should have told her the amount was heavy so she could find another way.

28

PACKING

When I was at primary school my father went on business trips five or six times a year and each trip lasted for at least one month. Each time he always had one suitcase and one black office bag for his trip. In the suitcase he only put a few clothes. The T-shirts were all white. The pants were all black or deep blue. And the one or two sweaters were all light colored. He used to fold each piece carefully without any wrinkles. He used to bring a big pile of money with him.

And he always put the money in the middle of the clothes layers. I remember he told me that people would not get the money out even when they used knives to stab his suitcase. If he took a plane he normally just locked the suitcase with a lock but if he took a train he normally took a huge and thick chain with him. He said the chain was to lock the suitcase on the rack in case people took the suitcase while he was sleeping. It seldom took my father more than thirty minutes to pack up his suitcase.

北京小孩

While he was packing, I just stood beside him, seeing him pulling out a suitcase either from the top of a closet or from under the bed, placing the suitcase on the bed, opening it with a sharp and clear sound from the snap, unzipping the suitcase with his right hand. He then opened his closet and his drawers, moved the clothes to the bed, stretched them first, folded them, with two hands holding them, placed them in the suitcase, and cleared the wrinkles. He seldom took any towels, toothbrush, or soap with him. But he always brought his own big mug, and normally kept it in his office bag. His mug was nothing more than a fruit jar but with the cover made by his elder sister. I remember he only packed up his suitcase a few hours before setting off.

When I grew up and took my own trips I always made a list of the things that I needed to pack and my father always laughed when he saw I was making the list. I once asked him why but he did not say anything, just laughed. He had stopped his business trips since I was in middle school. He used to unpack my back-pack or suitcase which I had already packed one week before my trip. My own packed bag always looked very crowded and there were always one or two things I could not put in. Besides clothes I used to take my own sheet, towels, and toothbrush. And I used to have some milk and some snacks in my bags. Each time after my father's packing the stupid looking luggage became slim and nice. I asked my father how he did this. He said he just made everything flat to lie in the bag or suitcase. He said to me sometimes standing and being tall did not work. He was joking with me as I used to complain that I was not as tall as a volleyball or basketball player.

北京小孩

I seldom kept money in my bag as I was always afraid that my luggage would get lost. I insisted that I should carry the money with me. Seeing no chance of persuading me to change my mind, my father asked his elder sister to make two wide belts with pockets for me. He told me to put the money in the pockets and tie the belt at my waist under my clothes.

When I was at university my father always offered to help me with the packing but I refused by saying that I wanted to do it by myself. I also stopped him by saying that he did not know what I was to pack and I would not be able to find something if he packed for me. He did not say anything except "You have grown up." I normally replied with a simple phrase "of course". First he stayed and watched me packing up my stuff but I always asked him to leave me alone. He seldom said anything but left quietly. And he always asked me when he was about to leave, "So I am leaving?" I replied by saying "yes" without looking at him. Later my father stopped coming to my place when I was doing the packing up. But he always came after had I finished my packing. Although he did not say anything or do anything he always lifted my packed luggage, looked at it and then put it down. I did not stop him at all. Instead I felt that if he asked me if I wanted him to do the packing I would definitely say yes. But he never asked and I never told him until I was about to go to England to continue my studies.

It was one month before I went to England. After dinner my father casually asked me if I had gotten everything for my one year in England. I said yes. I hesitated to ask him if he could do the packing for me. He seemed to have something on his mind. He looked at me for several seconds and then asked, "Do you want me to help you with the packing?" "I want you to do it for me." I said without any hesitation.

On the following morning, my father came to my apartment in Zaojunmiao. I told him that I could only have thirty five kilos for the big suitcase. I said I had no idea what I could and should bring. I showed him my list. He crossed out some clothes, added some medicine. He used a scale to weigh the empty suitcase. He took down the measured weight. He put in a pillow cover, bed sheet, quilt cover, two sweaters, three jeans, one winter coat, one pair of winter boots, seven sets of underwear, a load of medicine, electrical plugs, and one pair of chopsticks. He closed the suitcase, and weighed it again. It was twenty kilos. So he opened the suitcase, added three T-shirts, two microwave boxes, a cooking knife, ten bottles of contact lens moisture, and closed the suitcase and weighed it again. It was twenty nine kilos. He then put in some cotton socks, and a Chinese-English dictionary, and face creams. It was thirty three kilos. He then added a bunch of pens. It was thirty five kilos.

He hesitated, wondering if the scale was accurate or not. He took the suitcase to a pharmacy nearby and weighed it there. When he came back, he decided to take out some cotton socks. He put the suitcase on the scale. It was thirty-four kilos. He said, "It is done." It took him the whole morning to do the packing. And it was the first time that I saw him sweat.

I do not know how he could manage to put all these things into the suitcase. When I went to Canada from England I only had a few more books to add but I had to get two suitcases as I could not close the suitcase even with the things that I brought from Beijing. I broke the zipper. I wish my father would have been with me.

北京小孩

179

29

HAIR

As always after taking a shower, I look at myself in the mirror. It is the same face as the one that I had when I was a child. But it is definitely not the same. I have many spots but I did not have any when I was a child. I have wrinkles but I did not have any when I was child. I have dry eyes but my eyes were shining when I was a child. But the only thing that remains the same is the hair and the style of the hair.

I used to have short hair, parted on the left side. My grandmother said to me when I was born I had hair on my head. She thought I would have very very thick, coarse and dark hair. But it turned out my hair is thin, soft and yellowish brown. She said my hair was like hers instead of my parents, both of whom had thick, coarse and dark hair at that time.

My grandmother had long hair down to her waist. She had a yellow wooden comb. Every morning the first thing after she got up was to stand at the door, lower her head to one side, and comb her hair gently. I remember her hair was mixed with dark and gray colors even when she was in her 70s. She did not have any hair fall out. Because her hair was thin when she combed it her hair was like a piece of pure silk, very very smooth. I always stood beside her and asked to comb her hair for her. She always stopped me by saying one day when I grew up I would comb my hair and she would teach me to comb my hair. After she combed her hair, she always turned her hair into a knot and bound it at the back. Then she put a big but very thin metal comb around her head. Then she looked at herself in the mirror, with two hands holding the short hair back and started her day.

She did not wash her hair every day. She only washed it once a week. She did not have any shampoo and probably she did not know what shampoo was. She only used soap, the soap that she used to wash clothes for her hair. When she washed her hair, I always put my fingers into her hair. Her skin was soft. And her hair was smooth. I could have my fingers falling from the top of her hair to the end without moving my fingers. I liked to see the white foam on her hair. She did not use too much soap. She only used soap on the top of her head and then let the soap foam spread to her hair. The foam was big and white, like the foam from the sea.

After she rinsed her hair, the gray hair turned dark. It was so amazing to me. And when I told her that her hair changed colors she always laughed and said to me, "I am getting old. When I was young, like you, I had soft and yellowish brown hair." She had never had a hairdryer. She always used a towel to dry her hair. And then she asked me to use the yellow wooden comb to comb her hair. I could see a clear parting line on her head. And it was on the left. I said to her, "Nanny, your hair parts on the left. So does mine." And she always laughed with one arm around me and said, "That's why you are my granddaughter." I liked combing her hair. The comb would fall naturally without using any strength. The hair still looked dark and it was shining.

I asked my grandmother why I had short hair. I said to her I wanted to have long hair. Each time she always turned to me, looked in my eyes and said, "You will. You will. When you grow up I will comb your hair for you. Girls always have long hair. And it is girls that let their hair grow. You can do a lot of things with long hair. And it is nice to have long hair on your wedding."

At that time my mother said my hair was long. It was above the neck. I always imagined that I had long hair. I used to ask my grandmother to lend me her big hair comb and clipped the towel to my hair with it. I used to ask my grandmother to lend me her yellow wooden comb and combed the towel as if it was my hair.

I had never had a comb until I first had the chance to have long hair. It was when I was twelve.

One day I told my grandmother that I wanted to have long hair. I said to her that all the girls in my class had long hair and they all could use beautiful hair bands in their hair. My grandmother touched my hair and said: "You can have it when you grow up. It is nice to have long hair when you grow up." I did not understand why she stopped me from having long hair.

I told my parents and my mother said I could if I wanted to but my father said it was better to have short hair. I was surprised by their answers as I thought my father would say yes and my mother would say no.

I started to let my hair grow. My grandmother got many small hair clips for me and a lot of hair bands for me also. Some were pink, some were yellow, some were in the shape of butterflies and some were in the shape of flowers. And for the bands, some were green cloth bands, and some were a cluster of plastic pearls of different colors and some were like combs in the shape of the moon with shiny pieces on the top. Because my hair was short I always put all the hair clips on my head and looked like someone who was selling hair clips. But I was so happy that I could have long hair.

But each time when I was busy with putting in the hair clips my grandmother started by being happy but ended crying when helping me to fix my hair with these clips. I asked her why. She did not tell me.

My mother used to say that I looked like a stupid village girl with all these ugly hair clips. And she said it made her sick when she saw I had my hair bound back with my hair band. She said it was like the tail of a sheep. And she could grab my hair when she was angry with me. And one day she said to me seriously that because I spent too much time on my hair my study had been affected. She was right that for the midterm exam I was not ranked as the first in my class as before. I was the second. She said I should have my hair cut. I said no. I promised that I would work hard and asked her to let me keep my hair growing. She said to me, "No."

I told that to my grandmother. She did not say anything but gave me a pink butterfly comb with transparent silk on the top and shiny pearls on the side. She used it to comb my hair and bound my hair with it. She then held my face and looked at me, "You will have long hair but it should be when you grow up. And I will comb your hair on your wedding. It is nice for girls to have long hair and it is nice for girls to get married with long hair." I nodded.

On the following day my mother took me to take a bath. Normally I took a bath at home or at her school. But this time she took me to a public bath near Xizhimen. After the bath, she put me on a cold huge leather seat. A hairdresser came. My mother said, "Cut it short.'" I heard the hairdresser say to my mother, "Her hair is very soft, thin and the color is nice. It would be better to let it grow longer." "Cut it to short," my mother said. My hair tumbled down to the floor.

One year later my grandmother died. And my hair was no longer than that of the boys in my class.

I had never let my hair grow until I was at university. There were many many times that people wondered if I was a boy. And I was proud of this.

30

SANGE

I did not know that my father's cousin had three boys until one day there was a quarrel between one of our neighbors and my father's cousin's wife, my aunt. I do not remember what the neighbor said but I remember my aunt cried when the neighbor said, "You are so great that you have a son like Xiaosan." I remember my aunt ran to her house with a big bang of the door and the crash of something dropping on the floor.

My father told me Xiaosan was their youngest son who was put into prison for years when he was a teenager. My father said it was because he was a thief. My father told me not to tell anyone about Xiaosan and I should never mention Xiaosan in front of my aunt and her family.

Two years later on a summer morning, I heard my grandmother and my mother talking to someone outside. I opened the door and saw that my aunt and a young man were talking to my mother. "Do you still remember him?" my aunt asked me. I shook my head. He was very very dark. His hair was very very short and it seemed he just had shaved his head. His teeth were extremely white. There was something shining but also strange and uncertain in his eyes. He had a black cat in his hands. "It is your Sange (third elder brother)," said my grandmother. "You do not remember him?" I still shook my head. "She was too young," said my aunt. "Do you remember her?" she asked my "Sange". "I wouldn't be able to recognize her if I met her on the street, but now I can say I remember what she looked like when she was young. She did not change at all," said my Sange. I laughed. I was twelve at that time.

No one during the conversation really told me that he was just released from prison and no one mentioned where he had been for all the years that had passed. I remember the only sentence which suggested what my Sange had done was from my mother. "So be good since you are out." No one made any comments. I only heard the cat made a noise as my Sange stroked it with strength.

I always met my Sange every morning as I went to school at 7 or 7:15am. And every morning he was sitting on the bank of the Gaoliang River with his cat in his hands. He always smiled at me and asked me if I wanted him to take me to school and I always said no. He then waved his hand to me and said, "Be a good student. Do not play truant." And every day at noon when I came back, he was still sitting there in the sun. The cat was still in his hand. "You finished school?" he asked. I nodded. "Did you learn anything?" I nodded. "Is it good?" I still nodded. "Go home to get your lunch. Do not let me keep you. Otherwise you will be late for the class in the afternoon." I nodded and ran to my house. When I turned toward him at the corner I saw he was standing there, waving his hand to me. And then I heard the voice from the cat, a long and sharp voice. I was scared.

When I went to school again after lunch, Sange was still there. "Going to school?" he asked again. I nodded my head. "When will you be back?" "I do not know. Sometimes around 4pm and sometimes around 5pm." "Do not be late for school." He then let me go.

The same dialogue happened again when I was back. And it repeated for a few weeks.

There were several times that I wanted to talk to him. I wanted to tell him not to sit in the sun. I wanted to tell him to get a hat if he was sitting in the sun. But I never never talked to him as my mother told me many times to keep away from him.

I remember I once asked my grandmother how my Sange became a thief. My grandmother did not give me

北京小孩

189

any answer but a long and deep sigh. "His fate is too bitter, too bitter," she said and it was the only sentence she said to me.

Later I knew that my Sange was very smart but not very obedient. My aunt and uncle had very high expectations of him as their first two sons did not go to university. The eldest son became a painter and the pride of the family. They were very strict to my Sange and they beat him up very often and one day my Sange ran away. No one knew where he was until one day they were told that he was arrested and put into prison. And from then on, my uncle had decided that he did not have this son and no one in the family was allowed to mention my Sange's name. I still do not know what his name was except "Xiaosan".

One morning I got up very very early. I went to the river and I saw my Sange was there. I sat beside him. We were silent for a long time before he started to talk. "Heizi is my only friend. They wanted to skin it and eat it because there was no meat. I fought with them. I could not loose Heizi. He is my only friend. He can understand me. No one loves me. No one cares about me. They treat me as rubbish. I want to be good and I have decided to lead a life like anyone else. But they do not want me to change. I want a job. I can sweep the street. I can clean the public toilets. I can do everything. But they won't give me any chance. They won't." He cried. And the cat, Heizi, looked at him, stared at him, using his feet to touch his arm. I was trying to say something to him but what he said afterwards scared me. "They won't give me a chance. They won't let me change and they won't let me be a good man. I won't let them be happy. I will make them regret their decision!'" He said so firmly and he stroked Heizi so heavily that Heizi tried to escape but he pushed Heizi back to his hand and pushed its head down to its neck. I heard a big moan from Heizi. I then ran all the way to my house.

In the evening I heard my grandmother say that my Sange's cat was missing and no one knew where it was. "The child's fate is too bitter, too bitter," she said.

北京小孩

I still met my Sange every day at the same time. He still smiled, talked and waved his hands at me. But Heizi was not in his hands anymore. And each time there was always a fear coming to my mind.

191

On one evening at the end of summer as I was washing the mop at the river bank, my Sange came to me. He was standing behind me and I saw his image on the river. I raised my head and looked at him. He did not say anything but grabbed the mop. I was shocked. I did not know what he would be doing. He took the mop and walked to my house. "Let me do this. Let me do this. I can do something. I can do something." My grandmother called my aunt and my aunt just stood quietly at the door. I saw she cried. Her tears fell down on the front of her blouse and she turned away and ran to her house with a big bang of the door. I left as well.

My Sange disappeared for a few months until winter came. And this time he brought a girl. She was very very large, twice as large as my Sange. She always spoke loudly. My Sange brought her to my house and told my grandmother the girl was his girlfriend and they planned to get married early next year. "That's good.

That's good," my grandmother said happily. From then on I seldom saw my Sange. And my mother told me that he spent the whole time with the girl. My grandmother said my aunt worried that something might have gone wrong but she hoped that my Sange really had a good girl and would get married. "The child's fate is bitter. The child's fate is bitter."

The last time that I heard about my Sange was on one morning at the end of winter. My mother told me that he was arrested and put into prison again. She said this time the girl and the girl's family were all thieves. She said they were a gang of thieves. She said this time he was given a life sentence.

No one has ever mentioned him and the word of Xiaosan disappeared.

31

北京小孩

GARDEN

When I was a child, vegetables, fruit trees and flowers were grown in the garden in front of my house, in a village called Toudui Village along the Gaoliang River.

We used to grow tomatoes, chives, cucumbers, and garlic in the garden. In the morning I followed my grandmother to work in the small field to loosen the soil, and water the vegetables. And in the afternoon I followed my grandmother to inspect the vegetables.

When it was harvest time, I carried my small basket, following my grandmother to pick up the tomatoes and cucumbers. And I normally picked up the reddest tomato and put it into my grandmother's mouth. But she never ate it. She pretended it was very very nice but she did not want to eat it. She asked me to taste the tomato. And when we picked up the cucumbers she used her clothes to wipe them, put them into my mouth, and looked at me with smiles on her face.

北京小孩

194

We used small knives to cut the chives. I was lazy so I did not bend down myself. I just used my hands with my back straight. Sometimes I broke the chives into two parts. My grandmother used to joke by saying that we had left the rest in the field for next year. Once we had collected the chives she crushed them with ginger, spring onions, and salt, and steamed them altogether. So when winter came we could have the chives for our meals.

We used to have three persimmon trees and one date tree in the garden. I was the one who always climbed the persimmon trees to pick the persimmons when winter came. My grandmother was the one that stood under the trees. Sometimes when I broke a branch, she was scared that I might fall down to the ground.

We used to have flowers during most days of the year. I liked watering flowers in the morning and in the evening. My grandmother bought a small rabbit-shaped pot for me to water the flowers. I remember my first photo was when I was watering the flowers with my grandmother sitting beside me. I was six at that time.

One of the flowers that we had is one that could be made to dye my nails. My grandmother used to pick them in the morning, crush them with a small brown mortar and pestle, and dye my nails in the afternoon. I liked to look at my colorful nails. I asked my grandmother why she dyed my nails. She said she wanted me to look pretty. I said to her that I wanted to dye hers but she said she was too old and she would die one day. I then put my arms around her neck and said, "No. I do not allow you to die. And you will not die."

But she still died. And we had only the fruit trees left.

Later my father bought two puppies for me.

195

32

MOTHER

Today my mother cried. She cried in front of me. She cried bitterly. She said she could not understand why her life was always so hard.

She said to me her parents died when she was at middle school. She said she grew up in her sisters' and brother's families. She said when she was a student she was always afraid of summer and winter vacations while others were happy because did not need to go to school but stayed at home. "I did not have my own home. I had nowhere to go. I spent one week at one of your aunts' homes and one week at the other of your aunt's homes, and then one week in your uncle's home and one week in one of my classmates' homes," she said and cried. "Everyday was like a whole year. It is not my own home. I have never known what the love from parents means." She was still crying.

I remember one of my aunts told me when my mother was little she had a terrible disease. My uncle's wife did not want to look after my mother and threw her out of the door. My aunt said to me that she picked up my mother and put her in her arms and hugged her. My aunt said to me because she was sold by my mother's parents because of their poverty she could not bring my mother home. My aunt, the girl-wife, had to look after the family into which she was sold. She said to me, "Your mother had a very very hard life, a very very hard life."

My mother said since she married my father in 1976 she had been doing whatever to keep the family together. She said because she had never had a real family she wanted me to have real family, to have all the love that she had never had. She said when she found out she was pregnant with me she chose to stay in Haidian Hospital. "It is eight months. I just wanted to keep you. I did not want to lose you. Do you understand?" She said she stayed in bed all the time as she did not dare to move. She said she was afraid if she moved she would lose me.

She said when the doctors took me out I did not cry and she worried that I was dead. "Your body was dark but your face was purple. The doctor patted you on your back and you started to cry. And you had hair on your head. It was very very soft," she said.

"When you were little, you were looked after by your grandmother. I had no choice. I had to work and care for the family. Your father was busy and he did not come home very often." I remember my father said to me that my mother was the one that carried the bricks and built the kitchen on her own when I was only two. And I remember my father once told me that at that time I was able to stand beside my mother and pass her the broken bricks. And I suddenly remember all of these things and I felt I was back at the age of two.

199

It was very very hot that summer. My mother was carrying bricks with a one-wheeled cart and I was running after her, standing beside her. I remember that my mother was putting a towel around her neck while picking up a brick from the cart and mixing it with concrete. And occasionally she asked me to look for small pieces of brick for her. I remember that I used all my strength to pick up a brick and when I was ready to pass it to my mother it fell. It fell on my feet and I cried.

I also remember when I was a child my mother was the only one that went to the gas station near Beifang Jiaotong University to renew the bottle of gas and the only one that brought hundreds of kilos of Chinese cabbages from a market near Xizhimen back home on her bike before winter came.

She rode a big black men's bike. She hooked the bottle of gas on the back of her bike. When she rode she could not keep her balance and the bike was always moving. I remember my mother said to me and my grandmother many times as a joke that people working at the gas station always asked her why she was the only one that renewed the bottle of gas. And my mother always told them that my father worked in another province. And I remember my mother always said to me and my grandmother, "What else could I tell them? My husband does not work in Beijing!" She then became very very silent.

I also remember every year before winter came my mother always went to the market to buy at least 200 kilos of Chinese cabbages. She always piled several dozen Chinese cabbages up on a piece of plank on the back of her bike. She started transporting the Chinese cabbages in the afternoon until the late evening. And I remember my grandmother and I were moving them from the yard to the corridor. When my mother had finally transported all the Chinese cabbages to the house, because of the cold weather her face was extremely red, and her nose which was higher and straighter than most Chinese was like a red carrot, and her fingers, which were thick and short, were swollen. But she never had a rest. She always packed the Chinese cabbages with waste newspapers and piled them around the corner. And she never never complained that she was the only one in the family that had done this for nearly twenty years. She has not complained.

"I know that I have been very strict with you. I beat you and scolded you. But it is just because I wanted you to be good and to be successful," she said. "And it is because I am your mother. I have spoiled you." She paused and looked at me. Her eyes were red and full of tears. Her face is full of wrinkles. Her hair is getting whiter though she dyed her hair very often. My mother is getting old. She used to be very pretty when she was young. People who knew her when she was young said she was like a movie star, slim, tall, and pretty. She is not tall any more. Her back is slightly bent. Her eyes are not full of light any more. Blood is seen in her eyes. She is getting old and it is just because of me. It is just because of me.

My mother continued to say that she was proud of me when I was at school. She said I was always the best in my class and in my school. "You think I was too strict with you. I just did not want you to become arrogant. I wanted you to understand that there would always be someone else who was much better than you. You hate me and I know this. But there is not any single mother who would want to see her own child be a failure. You did not understand. And you still do not understand," she sighed.

"When you were in university, you were ill. You only remember how miserable you were. But do you know how sad I was? Do you know how much you hurt me by losing your temper with me?

"Because of your illness your temper was terrible and you said a lot of terrible things to me. You even asked me to leave the family just because I said something that I had no idea why I was wrong. Where could I go? I have no family. If I had my mother and father alive I would cry to them. But they left me when I was little. You are my daughter. But you treated me like

北京小孩

a dog. I am your mother. I am not a stranger. How can you treat me like a dog?

"Do you know how hurtful your father has been to me because of you? And most times I have not done anything wrong. I have not done anything wrong to you and your father. I have not. Do you know these things? You don't!

"And your father even decided to leave the family because of another woman! Do you know how I felt? You do not!"

"Mum, I know. I know. I am wrong. I am wrong. Please forgive me. I promise that I will never never do it again."

"There have been many times that I wanted to die. If I die I would not suffer all of these things. But once I thought about the family, your father and you, I did not want to die. I know if I die everyone would laugh at you and you won't be able to be alive. You do not want people to say that because of you I have died, do you? If I die, what can you say to our neighbors, your aunts and my colleagues? Are you going to tell them that you made me die? You really do not understand these things. You do not." My mother was choking.

I stared at her. I did not know what I could say.

"You do not know there have been many times that I had heart problems after your father lost his temper with me and after you said terrible things to me. But I told myself that I should not die. I should not let others laugh at us. You do not want your face but I want to keep my face. There is no one that I could talk to. There is no one. I can only swallow all the bitterness myself. When can you understand me?"

She wiped her tears and continued. "Once you started working, you still did not make life easy for us. You did not get along with your colleagues. You always thought you were somebody and you did not to listen to your supervisors. And you did not know how much I worried about this. You did not know and you do not know.

"Then you went to Sheffield and then Montreal. But you did not know how much I worried about you. For the first week I could not eat and I could not sleep. When I knew that you did not have enough money I did not know what I could do. Your father decided to send some money to you so you could live better. We were happy when you said you knew some people there but you did not know how much I worried that your study would be affected. You did not know how much I worried that you would not get your degree..." I just listened, and listened quietly.

"You do not know how much I have worried about you. You do not know," she suddenly raised her voice. "I know. I know it all," I said.

北京小孩

ABOUT THE AUTHOR

Wei Su is a recent Sauvé Scholar-in-Residence at McGill University in Montreal. She holds a Masters in Print Journalism from Sheffield University in the U.K. and is a graduate of Beijing University of Aeronautics and Astronautics. For three years she was a features writer for *Beijing Today*. She has also held a senior position in China in marketing and branding. Ms Su currently lives in Shanghai where she is writing subsequent stories of her coming-of-age to include her university, working and postgraduate years.

Author contact: suweiinbeijing@yahoo.com

Printed in the United Kingdom
by Lightning Source UK Ltd.
132620UK00001B/274-276/A